French & Spanish
Made Easy

2 Books in 1

French + Spanish. The Quick &

Funny Way To Learn Foreign

Languages

By Carol Carlson

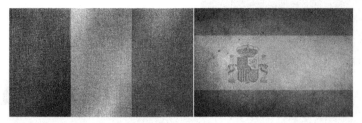

French

Made

Easy

---

*Learn French Fast with Short Stories &
Common Phrases for Beginners. Improve
Grammar & Vocabulary to Become Fluent in
Conversational Dialogue. Speak and
Understand French Step-by-Step*

By Carol Carlson

3

Table of Contents

Introduction

Welcome to *French Made Easy,* a book that has been designed for you to learn French effectively and with ease. This book will touch on everything you need to know about the French language, and by reading this book, you will gain a strong foundation to begin using the French language. This book contains everything from the structure of a sentence to pronunciation and common uses of the language like how to order in a restaurant and how to book a hotel room. Taking this book with you on your travels to a French-speaking place will give you all of the tools you need to get around easily, make all of your travel arrangements, and even have casual conversations with locals. To begin, I will share with you some tips that will help you to learn the French language most effectively.

When learning a new language, it is important to read about pronunciations and the combinations of letters as well as how to say them. The benefit of the French language compared to English is that they both use the same alphabet, so this will make it easier for you when looking at completely new words. The thing that may become tricky, though, is that the pronunciation of most of the letters is different from the pronunciation in English. There are some letters whose pronunciation remains the same, though. We will look at this more in-depth in the first chapter of this book.

Once you are aware of how to pronounce each of the letters in the French language and common letter pairings that you will come across, it is important to read the words you are learning aloud. Doing this makes learning much easier, as the vocalization of the word will make your brain more likely to remember it. Not only is your brain processing the look of the letter (the combination of letters), but it is processing the sound of the word as well, as it comes out of your mouth. By only reading the word in your head, you are missing out on a whole other part of the language, which is the speaking portion. Unless you are working in a job that requires you to write French often, most of the time, you will be speaking the language aloud, so it is important that you learn how to do this at the same time as you are learning things like common French verbs or nouns. As you read through this book, I recommend you take a few seconds to read the new words you learn aloud three or four times over to solidify them in your memory and to practice the pronunciation of them.

When learning a new language, there will be an accent that goes along with this that is likely different from the accent you use when you speak your native language. This will be something that comes with practice, but being aware of this is important. When you read the letters in a word in French, you will do so in a different accent than you would if you were reading in English. The same goes for speaking. While at first, it may be quite obvious that you are new to the language, in time your accent will develop along with your language skills. The French accent is something that we will talk about in the first chapter of this book, but until then keep in mind that this will differ from the accent we use when speaking English.

The chapters in this book have been laid out strategically so that you are learning certain things after others, as many of these topics build on other ones. Reading this book in order is necessary to get the most out of it for this reason. The first few chapters are in place to give you the basics of forming a sentence and pronouncing words in French, after which we move on to real-world examples of where you will see and use these rules you have been taught. After you have gone through the book once in order, at least, then you can come back to any chapter you need to spend more time on, but I recommend reading it at least once all the way through in order first.

Another tip for learning a new language is to ensure that you are exposing yourself to the language often enough. If you are leaving a week or two in between your language studies, it will be as if you are starting over every time you come back to learn more. Your tongue and brain may have forgotten the pronunciation, and you will have to spend a large chunk of time reviewing. This can cause you to become discouraged as you may think that you are not picking up the language, and you may then stop your studies altogether. In reality, though, the problem is frequency not your ability to pick up and remember the language. To avoid this from happening, it is important that you expose yourself to the language at least once every day or two. Preferably every day. This doesn't have to be dedicated to studying, it can be listening to a podcast that is in French or watching a French movie with English subtitles, or French subtitles even. It could also be trying to read a chapter of a book, an article online in French, or talking to a friend in French. Any of these things mentioned will expose your brain to the language, and this will keep your knowledge of it at the forefront of your mind. As you go about your life, there are many things that your brain is processing, and the longer you go between French exposures, the more likely you are to forget what you have learned. Your brain needs to make room for new knowledge, and it does this by forgetting things. By exposing yourself to a little bit of the new language every day, you are keeping it relevant.

The French language is one of the most commonly used in the world and is the only language (other than English) that is spoken in every single continent of the world. There are places in Africa, in South America, North America, and beyond that speak French as a first or second language. This makes it so useful to learn and to know how to speak it. If you are travelling, the chances that you will come across French on street signs, pamphlets, and brochures or when speaking to someone new are very high. By deciding to learn this language you are giving yourself quite an advantage as an international traveller. This will not only make travelling easier, but it will give you the ability to meet and connect with so many more people, which you otherwise wouldn't have been able to communicate with.

Chapter 1: Pronunciation

In this first chapter of the book, we are going to explore the alphabet and how to pronounce it, as well as some common pairings of letters that you will come across quite often and their pronunciations. This chapter will get you set up nicely for the rest of this book, where you will learn useful phrases and words.

The Alphabet

The first topic of discussion is the alphabet. The French alphabet is the same as the English language alphabet. If you are a native English speaker, it will be easier to learn French than it would be to learn a language like Russian or Mandarin Chinese, as these use symbols that you would have to learn from scratch. Because of this, you are already beginning part of the way through by knowing the alphabet!

This alphabet used in French, English and a variety of other languages, comes from the Latin alphabet. There are 26 letters in total, each with an uppercase and a lowercase form.

Though the alphabet used in French is the same as that used in English, the pronunciation of some of the letters is quite different. The twenty-six letters are below, with the accompanying pronunciation in brackets beside them;

A (ah)

B (bay)

C (say)

D (day)

E (euh)

F (ef)

G (jh-ay)

H (ash)

I (ee)

J (jh-ee)

K (kah)

L (el)

M (em)

N (en)

O (oh)

P (pay)

Q (koo)

R (err(roll the r))

S (ess)

T (tay)

U (ooh)

V (vay)

W (doo-bl-uh-vey)

X (ee-ks)

Y (ee-greck(roll the r))

Z (zed).

As you can see, here are a few letters whose pronunciations remain the same, like the following letters: f,l,m,n,o, and s. All of the other letters, however, will have new pronunciations. Study them and learn their new pronunciations by speaking them aloud a few times over before moving onto the next chapter.

Common Letter Pairings And Their Pronunciations

As you know from speaking English, the pronunciation of the letters of the alphabet will change when placed together with other letters. We will look at the most common cases of this in this section, the ones that you will come across most commonly. Practice pronouncing these sounds aloud, just like you did for the letters of the alphabet above.

Ai [eh]

Au [oh]

Eau [oh]

Eu [uh]

Ei [eh]

In [eh]

Ien [yeh]

O [oh]

Ou [oo]

On [aw]

Om [aw]

Oi [wah]

Un [eh]

Ch [sh]

As you can see, sometimes different sets of letter combinations will produce the same sounds as each other, such as *on* and *om*, but you will see both just as often as each other in words. Further, some of these letter combinations and the sounds they produce are different from how they would sound in English, and some of them may not even exist in the English language.

Examples In Words

An example of the above combinations at work in a word is the word *Chaud* (*hot*). This word may seem like it would be pronounced like [sh-ah-ooh-day], according to the sounds of the letters themselves, but when the letters *a* and *u* are placed together in French, it is actually pronounced as [oh], as you can see in the list above. Therefore, the word *chaud* is pronounced *chaud [sh-o-d]*.

Voiture (car) may seem like it would be pronounced as [v-oh-ee-t-uh-r], but in fact, due to the letters *oi* being placed next to each other in this word, they are pronounced as a [wah] sound. Therefore, *voiture* is pronounced [v-wah-t-oo-r]

The Letter *S*

In French, the sound that an *s* makes will often change when it is placed beside a vowel. The example below demonstrates this.

Nous Avons

This phrase means *We have.*

Separately, these two words would be *nous* [new] and *avons* [ah-voh], but when they are together in a phrase, the combination of the *s* at the end of *nous* with the *a* at the beginning of *avons*, changes their pronunciation. This combination of the *s* and *a* makes them come together to form the *z* sound. So now, we would actually say it like this, *nous avons* [new-z-ah-voh]. The *s* that was silent in the word *nous* now comes out but in a different sound.

Keep this rule in mind whenever you see an *s* next to a vowel. It is less important when you are speaking slowly and saying only a few words at a time, but it is helpful to know when you are listening to someone else speak French, especially if it is a fluent and native French speaker. You will likely often hear the *z* sound and be wondering what word they said that had this letter in it. Knowing this rule, you will be able to determine that they were actually saying two words together and that the first one likely ended with the letter *s,* and the second began with a vowel. Understanding words like this will help you to understand native speakers and things like French films, and it will also help you to develop a good French accent of your own.

Another case where we can see this is in the following sets of words;

Vous Avez and *Vous Êtes*

These mean "you guys have" and "you guys are." The verb *Avez* means "to have," and the verb *Etre* means "you guys are."

How Pronunciation Affects Sentence Meaning

In some cases, the emphasis of the pronunciation differences that combinations of letters produce is very important to the meaning of your sentence. Below are two different statements that mean different things, and if we did not change our pronunciation of the words in the first example, (the one with an *s* and a vowel next to each other) like explained above, then we would be confusing people with what we were trying to say. You can see how this is the case below;

Ils Ont they have*[eel-z-oh]*
Vs.
Ils Sont they are *[eel][s-oh]*

The first example, *ils ont* means "they have," while the second example, *ils sont* means "they are." The pronunciations of these two are below;

Ils Ont [eel-z-oh]
Vs.
Ils Sont [eel][s-oh]

Notice how the first example would normally be pronounced as *ils ont [eel][oh],* but since we have the letter s next to a vowel, we would actually say *ils ont [eel-z-oh].* Without making this difference in sound that is caused by the s and the *o,* the person you are speaking to could have trouble determining which of these two statements you are saying. This could confuse the entire meaning of your sentence. Without the *z* sound, these two statements sound very similar to each other.

French Accents

In this section, we will look at the different types of accents that you will see above or below letters in French. You have likely seen this before when looking at French words, such as two dots over the letter *e.* We are going to look at all of the different types of accents and how they change the pronunciation of the letters that they are placed on.

The letter *e* is the most commonly used character in the entire French language. You will come across the letter *e* more than any other letter in the entire language. When it comes to the letter *e,* can be pronounced a lot of different ways. When you see an *e* with no accent, you sometimes wonder how it is pronounced, and you can look to the letters before and after it to get some clues. There is one way to find out exactly how to pronounce the letter *e.* If you see an accent over top of it, this will tell you exactly how to pronounce it, and there will be no more wondering. You can also find accents under or over top of the letters c, a, i, u, and o. These accents will change the sound of the letter in specific ways.

The Cédille (Ç)

The cédille is an accent that you see below the letter *c*. This accent will change the way the letter is pronounced. This makes it sound more like an *s*. You will only find the cedille with the letter c but not with any other letter. This will only be seen before a vowel, as this will make the s sound right before a vowel like, sa, so, su. For example,

Garçon [g-ah-r-son]

The Accent Aigu (é)

An accent aigu (é) is placed on top of the letter e. This accent will change the way the letter e sounds. It will make it pronounced more nasally. To say this sound, hold your tongue at the bottom of your mouth and keep it still while pronouncing the e sound nasally, and there you have it.

The accent aigu looks like this;

é

For example, the word écrire [ay-k-ree-r], which is a verb that means *to write*.

The Accent Circonflexe (Ê)

This accent is like a hat on top of a letter and can be found on all vowels (except y). It looks like the following;

â

Ê

î

ô

û

This accent doesn't quite change the way the letter sounds, but it changes the speed at which it is said. It makes it so that the letter is pronounced quicker and with more force. For example,

Poîntu [p-wa-n-too], which means pointy

Août [oo-t], which means August

The Accent Grave (È)

This accent can be found on top of an a, an e or an u. It is similar to the accent aigu, but it is in the reverse direction. You can see this below;

À

È

Ù

This accent changes the meaning of two words which are spelled the exact same way. For example,

Ou vs. Où

[oo] vs [oo]

The former means *or* and the latter means *where.*

La vs. Là

[lah] vs. [lah]

The former means *the* and the latter means *there.*

A vs. À

[ah] vs [ah]

The former means *have,* and the latter means *at* or *to.*

The Accent Tréma (Ë)

This accent is two small dots above the letter e, i, or u. This accent is used to show that the letter is on top of, and the letter immediately after it in a word is to be pronounced separately. Think of the word Noël [noh-el], which means Christmas. This separates the o sound from the e sound. Below you can see the accent on the three letters it can be found with;

Ë

Ï

Ü

The name Chloë is an example of this

As well as the word Jamaïque [jah-mah-ee-k] which is the French way of saying Jamaica.

Chapter 2: Structure Of A Sentence

In this chapter, we will take your knowledge a step further and examine the structure of a sentence. This includes things like nouns, adverbs, and adjectives. In French, there is a little more that goes into structuring a sentence than in English, as there are a few more rules and the order of words is quite specific. We will look into this in-depth in this chapter, and by the end, you will be quite comfortable with structuring your own sentences.

Articles

The first part of a sentence that we will look at are articles. Articles are words that are attached to nouns. In English, we use the words *the, an* or *a* in front of nouns. These serve to set up the listener or reader for what is coming next, whether it is something specific or general. For example, *the boy* or *a boy*.

In French, every word is assigned a gender. Now, this may sound odd, but it is true. Everything from a chair to a kettle and everything else in between has an assigned gender. This gender is not assigned for no reason. The gender of a word informs which of the forms of *the* or you will use when speaking about that word. The gender of a word does not change. In French, there are many different forms of the words *the* and *a,* and you will choose which of these you use according to the gender of the word about which you are speaking. As you learn French nouns, you will need to learn its gender along with it. The best way to do this is to learn the noun along with the article that accompanies it because this article will tell you the gender of the noun. In this section, we will look at all of the different articles you will come across and some examples of nouns you will see them with. In the section that follows, we will go deeper into our study of nouns because then you will understand the articles that you will see them with.

L'Article Defini

In English, we do not have feminine and masculine nouns, so when we are talking about **something specific,** we use the word to describe it. This is called the definite article or *l'article defini,* [l-ar-tee-k-le][day-fee-nee]. We will first look at the singular form before moving onto the plural form.

Singular Definite Article

Masculine, *le,* [l-uh]

Feminine, *la,* [l-ah]
Vowel or h, *l',* [l]

All three of these mean *the,* and this is where French gets more complicated than English. In English, you only need to know that *the* is used in definite cases. In French, you must know that it is definite as well as the gender of the thing you are describing.

When attaching an article before a verb that starts with a vowel or with the letter *h* (which is a silent sound in French), you will use the letter *L,* followed by an apostrophe. This is so that there isn't the awkward sound of two vowels together, as this would be difficult to pronounce properly.

Some examples of when each article, along with a word which matches its gender are below for you to practice saying and memorizing.

The game, *le jeu,* [l-uh][j-uh]
The casino, *le casino,* [l-uh][k-as-ee-no]
The table, *la table,* [l-ah][tah-b-l]
The cup, *la tasse,* [l-ah][tah-ss]
The bee, *l'abeille,* [l-ah-bay]
The hexagon, *l'hexagone,* [l-ex-a-gone]

Notice how the *l'* before a noun becomes blended into the noun itself when you are saying it aloud. Practice this a few times before moving on.

Plural Definite Article

In English, when we are speaking about a group of nouns in a specific way, we would still use the word. In French, there is a different definitive article (*l'article defini*) than those explained above (le, la, l') that are found with plural nouns.

Plural (either masculine or feminine), *Les,* [l-ay]

We will use the same article for plural nouns regardless of whether they are feminine or masculine. Some examples of this are below;

The books, *les livres,* [l-ay][lee-v-re]
The oranges, *les oranges,* [l-ay][oh-ron-j]

L'Article Indefini

We will now move on to the Indefinite Article, or *l'article indefini.* This is used when we are speaking about something unspecific, where in English we would say the word *a* or *an.*

We would use these to describe a noun in general instead of one specific item.

Singular

Masculine, *un,* [uhn]

Feminine, *une,* [oo-n]

A few examples of this are below,

An orange, *un orange* [uhn][oh-ron-j]

A book, *un livre,* [uhn][l-ee-v-r]

An apple, *une pomme,* [oo-n][p-uh-m]

Plural

When it comes to the plural form of unspecific or indefinite articles, there is not an exact equivalent of an article in English, but the closest thing would be when we use the word *multiple* or *many*. This is not an article by definition in English, but for our purposes, it will be.

Some, *des,* [d-ay]

Multiple books, *des livres,* [d-ay][l-ee-v-rs]

Many apples, *des pommes,* [d-ay][p-uh-m]

Notice how one of the above examples is feminine, and one of them is masculine (as we saw above with *un et une*), but when it comes to the plural form, they both are attached to the article *des*.

L'Article Partitif

The Partitive Article is used when we are talking about only a part of something, rather than the whole of it. This is often used when we are speaking about food. This is used when the noun is something we cannot count, which is why it is usually used with food.

Singular

In English, we would use the word *some* in this place. You will find examples of this below.

Masculine, *du,* [doo]
Feminine, *de la,* [d-uh][lah]
Vowel or h, *de l',* [d-uh][l]

Notice again how either starts with a vowel or the letter *h* (which would be silent), *de* is used, followed by the letter *l* and an apostrophe.

Some cheese, *du fromage,* [doo][fr-oh-mah-j]

Some pie, *de la tarte,* [d-uh][lah][tar-t]

Some money, *de l'argent,* [d-uh][l-ar-j-ont]

Plural

Plural Partitive Articles are used when we are talking about a portion of food that contains multiple items. Examples are below in order for you to better grasp this concept. Notice that this article is the same one used when speaking about indefinite items in multiples (as above).

Des, [d-ay]

Some Spinach, *des épinards,* [d-ay-s][eh-pee-n-ar-d]

Some Pasta, *des pâtes,* [d-ay][pah-t-s]

Nouns

We will now talk about nouns. As we know from speaking English, a noun is a *place,* a *person,* or a *thing.* If you know a few words from the French language already, many of these are likely nouns. If you know how to say chair or cereal, for example, these would be nouns. In the previous section, all of the words we attached to articles were nouns. There will be more pronunciation practice in this section, so continue to read the new words you learn aloud. The one major takeaway that you should get from this section is that in the French language, everything is gendered. Everything has a gender associated with it, just like you saw in the previous section. There is no trick that will tell you if a noun is feminine or masculine, you will have to remember this for the most part. To make this easier for you, as you are learning nouns they will all be paired with their appropriate article.

Before we get there, we will learn the French word for noun;

A Noun, un *nom,* [n-om]

Masculine and Feminine Nouns

As you know by now, there are some nouns that are feminine and some that are masculine, while others are plural. The articles that are placed with nouns are different depending on if the noun is masculine, feminine, or plural. Now that you are familiar with articles and the different forms and uses for them, we will look at some examples of nouns that use each of these articles. To help you remember which nouns are feminine and which are masculine more easily, we will now look at them in terms of the categories of nouns that tend to be feminine and others that tend to be masculine, so that you can group them in your brain and remember them later. Keep in mind, in the French language there will always be exceptions, but those will be learned later.

Feminine Nouns And Their Articles

We will begin by looking at the categories of nouns that contain feminine nouns. As you read through this section, read the nouns and their articles aloud to practice pronunciation.

School subjects are feminine, such as;
Chemistry, *la chimie,* [l-ah][shee-mee]
Gym, *la gymnastique* [l-ah][j-eem-nas-tee-k]
Language, *la langue* [l-ah][l-on-g]

Cars and car names are feminine. For example;
In French, there are two different words that mean car. They are both feminine nouns.
A car, *une auto* [oo-n][oh-toe]
A car, *une voiture* [oo-n][v-wah-too-r]
A Mazda 3, *la Mazda Trois,* [l-ah]Mazda][tr-wah](rolled r)

Most **foods that end with the letter *e*** are feminine nouns. For example;

A banana, *la banane,* [l-ah][bah-na-n]

A tomato, *la tomate,* [l-ah][t-oh-mat]

An apple, *la pomme,* [l-ah][po-m]

Continents are feminine nouns. For example;

Australia, *l'Australie,* [l-os-t-ra-lee]

Europe, *L'Europe* [l-you-rup]

Asia, *L'Asie,* [l-ah-see]

Mostly all **countries whose French names end with the letter *e*.** These are going to be feminine nouns. The countries below may not seem like they end with the letter *e*, but their French names do. For example;

France, *la France,* [l-ah][f-ron-s] (rolled r)

China, *la Chine,* [l-ah][sh-een]

Patagonia, *La Patagonie,* [l-ah][pat-a-go-nee]

Masculine Nouns And Their Articles

We will now look at some examples of noun categories that are masculine.

The **calendar** itself is a masculine noun as well as all of the **days in a week,** the **months** as well as the **seasons.** We will look at these nouns more in-depth in further chapters of this book, but keep this in mind until we get there.

Calendar, *le calendrier,* [l-uh][k-al-on-dree-ay]

December, *le décembre,* [l-uh][day-s-om-br-uh]

Summer, *l'ete,* [l-ay-tay]

Tuesday, *le Mardi,* [l-uh][mar-dee]

When speaking about a **specific date**, this is masculine. We will also look at these more in-depth in further chapters, starting with the basics, but keep this rule in mind as well.

June 6th, *le six juin,* [l-uh][s-ee-s][j-w-an]

October 12th, *le douze octobre,* [l-uh][doo-z][o-k-toh-b-ruh]

Colors are masculine nouns, as well.

Red, *le rouge,* [l-uh][roo-j]

Orange, *l'orange,* [l-oh-ron-j]

Pink, *le rose,* [l-uh][r-oh-z](rolled r)

Drinks are most often masculine.

Coffee, *le cafe,* [l-uh][k-af-ay]

Juice, *le jus,* [l-uh][j-oo-s]

Tea, *le the,* [l-uh][t-ay]

Foods that don't end with the letter *e* are masculine nouns.

Corn, *le mais,* [l-uh][mah-yee-s]

Sandwich, *le sandwich,* [l-uh][s-and-wee-ch]

Countries that end in any letter other than *e* are masculine nouns.

Canada, *le Canada,* [l-uh][k-ana-da]

Japan, *le Japon,* [l-uh][j-ap-on]

Directions on a compass are masculine nouns.

North, *le nord,* [l-uh][n-or]

South, *le sud,* [l-uh][soo-d]

East, *l'est,* [l-ess-t]

West, *l'ouest,* [l-oo-ess-t]

Languages are masculine nouns, although, as we saw above in the feminine noun categories, the actual school subject of languages and the word *language (la langue)* [l-ah][l-on-g] itself is feminine.

French, *le francais,* [l-uh][f-ron-say]

Greek, *le grec,* [l-uh][g-rek]

When we speak about **letters of the alphabet** on their own, these are masculine nouns.

A, *le a,* [l-uh][ah]

D, *le d,* [l-uh][d-ay]

P, *le p,* [l-uh][pay]

Plural Nouns

In the French language, some nouns are always plural and therefore are always associated with a plural article (les, des). While most of the time in English, a noun can be either plural or singular depending on what you are talking about, in French there are nouns that can only be used in a plural sense and therefore can only be used with a plural article. These plural nouns will either be accompanied by the article *les* or *des*. Examples of these can be seen below.

Business, *les affaires,* [l-ay][ah-f-air]

Asparagus, *les asperges,* [l-ay][ah-s-pair-j]

Luggage, *les bagages,* [l-ay][bah-g-ah-j]

Advice, *les conseils,* [l-ay][k-on-say]

All of these nouns will only be seen in their plural form. This is similar to the words *pants* or *glasses* in English. It is one item, but we talk about it as if it is more than one.

Pronouns

We will now move on to our study of another part of a sentence, the pronouns. Pronouns in French are called *les pronoms,* [l-ay][p-r-oh-no-m](rolled r). Pronouns are used English and French; in French, however, they have much more of an effect on the rest of the sentence than they do in English. In English, pronouns are things like: *I, we, they, she* and so on.

Personal Pronouns

Personal pronouns or, *les pronoms personnels,* [l-ay][p-r-oh-no-m][pair-s-on-el] are pronouns which are used in place of a grammatical person.

I, *Je,* [j-uh]
You, *Tu,* [too]
He, *il,* [ee-l]
She, *elle* [el]
We, on*, [oh-n](light *n* sound)
We, *Nous,* [new]
You (plural), *Vous,* [v-oo]
They (masculine or feminine), ***ils/elles,* [eel][el]

on is an informal pronoun that can replace *nous* to mean *we,* though the proper way to say *we* are by using *nous.*

** Notice that *'they'* has two different forms, one for masculine and one for feminine. Both French words for this (*ils* and *elles)* are pronounced in exactly the same way as their singular forms; *he* and *she* (il and elle), as the letter *s* is silent in these words.

Impersonal Pronouns

Impersonal pronouns or *les pronoms impersonnels* [eh-m-pair-soh-n-el] are pronouns that replace something in a sentence that is not a grammatical person. This could be a noun, an amount of something, a place, or a quantity. Examples are below.

This, *Ce,* [suh]
That, *ça,* [sah]
Multiple, *plusieurs,* [p-loo-see-uhr-s]
Who, *qui,* [k-ee]
What, *que,* [k-u-h]
Which One, *lequel,* [leh-k-el]

Adjectives

Adjectives or *les adjectifs* [l-ay][a-j-ek-teef] describe nouns. We use these in both French and English. Now that you are familiar with various French nouns and their articles, we will look at the adjectives that describe these nouns and more. Adjectives give a sentence more life, more description, and more life-like quality. These can be things like the color of something, the shape, the size or if it is ugly or pretty. In English, adjectives have only one form, but in French, they will have one of four forms.

Adjectives must be in agreement when it comes to the gender of the noun, and whether it is plural or singular, so we adjust the adjective to agree with this, just like we do with an article. The article of a noun will give you the information on how to make the adjective agree with the gender as well. The default form of every adjective in French is the masculine form, and from there we add letters to adjust the ending to make it feminine or plural or both.

Masculine	(nothing added)
Feminine	-e
Masculine plural	-s
Feminine plural	-es

We will now look at some examples of adjectives before adding them to nouns and adjusting their endings accordingly. As you read through these examples, say them aloud and practice the pronunciation.

Small, *petit* [p-uh-tee]
Big, *grand* [g-ron] (rolled r)
Ugly, *laid* [l-ed]
Sharp, *pointu* [pwa-n-too]
Hot, *chaud* [sh-oh]
Cold, *froid* [f-r-wa] (rolled r)

If the adjective ends with the letter -a, -e or -o, then both masculine and feminine form will be the same because we don't want to add another vowel (an *e)* on to the end of a word already ending in a vowel. Examples of this are below.

Damp, *humide,* [hoo-mee-d]
Masculine, *humide*
Feminine, *humide*
Masculine plural, *humides*
Feminine plural, *humides*

Try adding the appropriate endings to the example below using what you learned with the adjective *humide.*

Pretty, *belle* [b-el]

Masculine, *belle*

Feminine, *belle*

Masculine plural, *belles*

Feminine plural, *belles*

If the adjective ends with the letter -s or -x, then the masculine singular and masculine plural forms are the same. These adjectives are somewhat irregular, especially those ending in -x, so pay close attention. An example of this is below, and further is one for you to try.

Delicious, *Delicieux* [day-lee-s-yuh]

M: delicieux

F: delicieuse*

MP: delicieux

FP: delicieuses

*Notice how the -x has been removed and replaced by -se to make the feminine form. This is because 'delicieuxse' would not make much sense and would be a mouthful to try and say. We make it an adverb ending in -s and then add the appropriate feminine ending for both singular and plural feminine forms.

Try changing the endings of this adjective to make it in agreement with the gender. Be especially careful with the feminine forms; look above for assistance if need be!

Happy, *heureux,* [euh-ruh]
M: heureux
F:heureuse
MP: heureux
FP: heureuses

Surprised, *surpris,* [s-oo-r-pree]
M: Surpris
F; Surprise
MP: surpris
FP: surprises

Notice in this example how the masculine singular and plural forms are exactly the same.

We will now do a little practice on the things we have just learned about adjectives by combining it with what we know about articles and nouns. For each pair below, you can see them put together by adjusting the adjective to the gender of the noun.

The fairy and small, *La fée et petit,* **La** fée petit**e**

The apple and juicy, *La pomme et juteux, La pomme juteuse*

February and cold, *Le février et froid, Le février froid*

China and big/large, *La Chine et grand, La Chine grande*

The fairies and small, *Les fées et petit, Les fées petites*

Adverbs

Adverbs are another type of description word, much like adjectives. Adverbs can modify a verb, an adjective, and they can even modify themselves. There are different categories of adjectives, depending on the type of modification that they make. We will look at those different types now.

Frequency Modifications

The first type of adverb we will look at makes a modification in frequency. Some examples are below.

Ever, *jamais* [j-ah-may]

Rarely, *rarement* [r-are-mon]

Often, *souvent* [soo-von-t]

Always, *toujours* [too-joo-r]

Sometimes, *parfois* [par-f-wah]

Modifications Of The Manner In Which Something Is Done

The next type of adverb we will look at makes a modification in the manner in which something is done. Some examples are below.

Politely, *poliment* [poh-lee-mon]

Quickly, *vite* [vee-t]

Well, *bien* [bee-yeh]

Poorly, *mal* [mah-l]

Location Modifications

The next type of adverb we will look at makes a modification in the place in which something occurs. Some examples are below.

Outside, *dehors* [day-or]

Here, *ici* [ee-see]

There, *là* [lah]

Somewhere, *quelque part* [kel-kuh][par]

Modifications Of Amount

The next type of adverb we will look at makes a modification in the amount of something. Some examples are below.

Enough, *Assez* [ass-ay]

A lot, *beaucoup* [boh-koo]

little, *peu* [p-uhh]

Very, *tres* [t-ray]

Too Much, *trop* [t-r-oh]

Modifications Of Amount Of Time

The next type of adverb we will look at makes a modification in the time something takes, will take, or has taken. Some examples are below.

Soon, *bientot* [b-yen-toh]

Already, *deja* [day-j-ah]

Now, *maintenant* [man-tuh-nah]

A Long Time, *longtemps* [lon-g-tom-p]

Yesterday, *hier* [y-air]

Today, *aujourd'hui* [oh-j-oor-d-we]

Questioning Modifications

The next type of adverb we will look at makes a modification in terms of making something a question. Some examples are below.

How much, *combien* [k-om-b-yen]

Why, *pourquoi* [poor-k-wah]

When, *quand* [k-on]

How, *comment* [k-om-on]

Like (as an adverb, not a verb), *comme* [k-umm]

Negative Modifications

The next type of adverb we will look at is used to change something into the negative sense, or without instead of with. Some examples are below.

Never *ne... jamais* [nuh][j-am-ay]

Not *ne...pas* [nuh][pah]

Only *seulement* [s-uh-l-mon]

Not any more *ne... plus* [nuh][p-loo]

Comparison Modifications

The next type of adverb we will look at compares two things. Some examples are below.

Less, *moins* [m-wah-n]

More, *plus* [p-loo]

As well/Also, *aussi* [oh-see]

Superlatif Modifications

The next type of adverb we will look at speaks to the extremes of something. Some examples are below.

The most, *le plus* [luh][p-loo]

The least, *le moins* [luh][m-wah-n]

The best, *le meilleur* [luh][may-yur]

Prepositions

We will now move onto prepositions. These are other parts of speech that help you to accurately describe something. These are positioned after a noun, a verb, or an adjective in a sentence to describe the relationship between two things. In English, these are words like to, of, beside, behind, and so on. Prepositions can be tricky when relating them to English because many times, we must use them in a sentence when speaking French, whereas we would not use it in the same sentence when translated to English. Keep at it, and with practice, you will be an expert in no time. Below are the most common prepositions that you will use.

À [ah], *to, at, in*

Apres [ah-pray], *after*

Avec [ah-veh-k], *with*

Dans [d-ohn], *in*

Avant [ah-von], *before*

De [duh], *from, of, about*

Derriere [dare-y-air] *behind*

Entre [on-t-ruh] *between*

Par [pah-r], *by, through*

Pendant [pon-d-on], *as, while, during*

Pour [poo-r], *for*

Sans [s-on], *without*

Sous [s-oo] *under*

Sur [s-oo-ruh] *on, on top of*

Vers [v-air] *toward, near*

Practice these common prepositions and their pronunciation over and over aloud to get them solidified in your memory.

Look below at the example of prepositions in use to practice what you now know in a real example. We have already learned all of the parts of the sentence except for the verbs, which we will look at in the next chapter.

The boys walked quickly.
Ils ont marché vite.

With a sentence like this that includes a subject, an auxiliary, a verb, and an adverb, we can add a preposition onto it in order to relate it to a noun.

We are going to use the preposition *pendant,* which in English means *during.*

Ils ont marché vite *pendant*

Up until this point, our sentence reads; The boys walked quickly during. We now need a noun to attach to the end of this to make a full descriptive sentence. We are going to use the noun *la tempête* [tom-peh-te], which in English means *the storm.* So now we have;

Ils ont marché vite pendant la tempête.

Our sentence now reads, "the boys walked quickly during the storm. We now have a subject, an auxiliary, a verb, an adverb, a noun with its article. We have put together everything we have learned to form this beautiful and descriptive sentence. Say it aloud as many times as you can!

[eel][oh-nt][mah-r-sh-ay][v-ee-t][[pon-d-on][lah][tom-peh-te]

Ils ont marché vite pendant la tempête.

They walked quickly during the storm.

Study the following examples, referencing the list of prepositions above. All you need to know for this exercise is the following;

To run, Courir

To walk, Marcher

I ran toward McDonald's. J'ai couru vers McDonald's.

He walked behind her. Il a marché derriere elle.

I ran after him, J'ai couru après lui.

I walked through. J'ai marché par.

Chapter 3: Verbs

Verbs or *les verbes,* [lay][v-air-b], are the action words in a sentence. Just like in English, they describe an act of doing or the act of being. Verbs are arguably the most involved and most important part of speech. Verbs have to be adjusted in every sentence according to who or what they are in reference to and in what tense we are speaking. This adjustment of a verb is called *conjugation* (this word is the same in French and English). We will begin by looking at the most common verbs and their translations as well as their pronunciation, and then we will begin our lesson on verb conjugation.

To be, *Etre* [et-ruh](rolled r)

To have, *Avoir* [ah-v-war]

To go, *Aller* [ah-lay]

To Do, *Faire* [f-air]

To say, *Dire* [dee-r]

To know, *Savoir,* [sa-v-war]

To live, *Vivre* [vee-v-ruh]

To want, *Vouloir* [voo-l-war]

To see, *Voir* [v-war]

To hold, *Tenir* [tuh-neer]

To be able to, *Pouvoir* [poo-v-war]

Practice these verbs and their pronunciations before continuing onto the next section.

We will begin with the two most common verbs, *etre and avoir*. These verbs are the most commonly used in both French and English.

Present Tense Verb Conjugation
Avoir Et Être

We will begin with the verb *to have* or *etre*. Just like when we change a verb in English according to who we are talking about (I am, you are, she is, etc.) we do the same in French. Remember when we learned personal pronouns earlier in this chapter, this is where we revisit them. The example of this is below.

Verbe Etre: To be

Je suis	Nous sommes
Tu es	Vous etes
Il est	Ils sont
Elle est	Elles sont
On est	

Verbe Avoir: To have

J'ai*	Nous avons
Tu as	Vous avez
Il a	Ils ont
Elle a	Elles ont
On a	

*Je ai becomes j'ai because there are two vowels side-by-side.

While these two are the most common verbs, they are both what we call irregular verbs. This means they don't follow any sort of pattern, and you have to just memorize the conjugation of them. We will now look at the conjugation rules of regular verbs.

For regular verbs, you will take the verb down to its root. This means that you will take off its ending letters, and this will leave you with the root. Then, you add an ending that corresponds with the personal pronoun (the person that you are speaking about) and the tense in which you are speaking, and there you have a conjugated verb to add to your sentence.

Verbs can be classified into three groups;

1. Those which end in -er
2. Those which end in -ir
3. Those which end in -tir
4. Those which end in -re

I will give you examples of each of these so that you will know how to find the root of the verbs.

1. Those which end in -er

Jouer, *to play* [j-oo-ay]
Sauter, *to jump* [s-oh-tay]
Cacher, *to hide* [kah-sh-ay]

Je,   -e
Tu,   -e
il/elle/on, -e
Nous,   -ons
Vous,   -ez
ils/elles,   -ent

For these verbs, you will take off the -er, and you are left with the root: Jou, saut, cach. Then you add the endings and *voila!* You can see the examples of these conjugated below.

Jouer   **Sauter**   **Cacher**

59

Je joue   je saute   je cache

Tu joue   tu saute   tu cache

il/elle/on jouc   il/elle/on saute   il/elle/on   cache

Nous jouons   nous sautons   nous cachons

Vous jouez   vous sautez   vous cachez

ils/elles jouent   ils/elles sautent   ils/elles cachent

2. Those which end in -ir

For verbs that end in -ir, remove the last two letters to get to the root, then add the endings below, which differ based on the verb. We will look at the most common ones. Practice conjugating them and pronouncing them.

Finir, *to finish* [f-ee-near]

Je -is
Tu -is
il/elle/on -it
Nous -issons
Vous -issez
ils/elles -issent

Voir, *to see* [v-wah-r]

Je -is

Tu -is

il/elle/on -it

Nous -yons

Vous -yez

Ils/elles -ient

3. Those which end in -tir

Partir, *to leave* [par-tee-r]

Sentir, *to feel* [s-on-tee-r]

For verbs that end in *-tir,* take off all three of these letters to get to the root

Je -s

Tu -s

il/elle/on -t

Nous -tons

Vous -tez

ils/elles -tent

	Partir	Sentir

je	Pars	Sens
tu	Pars	Sens
il/elle/on	Part	Sent
nous	Partons	Sentons
vous	Partez	Sentez
ils/elles	Partent	Sentent

4.Those which end in -re

Vendre, *to sell* [von-d-r] (rolled r)

Rendre, *to return* [ron-d-r] (rolled r)

For verbs that end in -re, remove these last two letters and add on the endings below.

Je -s

Tu -s

il/elle/on -*

Nous -ons

Vous -ez

ils/elles -ent

*For verbs ending in -re, nothing is added to the end when you are using the personal pronouns of il, elle or on.

There is a verb that ends in -re that you may use quite often, though it is an irregular verb (like etre or avoir). This verb is conjugated differently.

Prendre, *to take* [p-r-on-d-r] (rolled r's)
When getting the root of this verb, you will take off the last three letters (-dre) to get the root word *pren*.

Je -ds
Tu -ds
il/elle/on -d
Nous -ons
Vous -ez
ils/elles -nent

While it is quite difficult to glean whether a verb is regular or irregular, a good rule of thumb is to try it out the regular way and if there is anything that sounds like too much of a mouthful, or if it has too many vowels too close together- it is likely conjugated in an irregular way. Like I mentioned previously, in French, we like to keep it flowing and sounding beautiful when we speak without much chance of a tongue-twister.

Below I will conjugate some more common verbs for you to see.

Aller, *To go*   Pouvoir, *To be able to*
    Savoir, *to know*

[ah-lay]   [poo-v-w-or]   [sah-v-w-or]

Je vais   Je peux
    Je sais

Tu vas   Tu peux
    Tu sais

Il/elle/on va   il/elle/on peut
    Il/elle/on sait

Nous allons   Nous pouvons
    Nous savons

Vous allez   Vous pouvez   Vous savez

ils/elles vont   ils/elles peuvent
    Ils/elles savent

Verb Conjugation In The Past Tense

When speaking in past-tense, you must still conjugate the verbs you are using just like you do when speaking in the present tense, but you will conjugate them in a different way.

The Past Participle

When we speak in the past-tense, we will change the verb we are using in order to communicate the fact that we are speaking about something that happened in the past. To do this, we will change the ending of the verb, just like we did when conjugating the present tense verbs, but we will change them in a different way. After we change the ending of the verb, the form is now called the Past Participle.

ER Verbs

We conjugate verbs that end in an -er by removing this ending and substituting it with an 'é.' Some examples are below;

Parler [par-lay], *to speak,* becomes Parlé [par-lay]
Aller [ah-lay], *to go,* becomes Allé [ah-lay]

Arriver [ah-ree-vay], *to arrive,* becomes Arrivé [ah-ree-vay]

Entrer [on-t-ray], *to enter,* becomes Entré [on-t-ray]

IR Verbs

We conjugate verbs that end in an -ir by removing this ending and substituting it with an 'i.' Some examples are below;

Finir [fee-nee-r], *to finish,* becomes Fini [fee-nee]

Mentir [mon-tee-r], *to lie,* becomes Menti [mon-tee]

Choisir [sh-wah-see-r], *to choose,* becomes Choisi [sh-wah-see]

RE Verbs

We conjugate verbs that end in an -re by removing this ending and substituting it with a 'u.' Some examples are below;

Vendre [v-on-d-ruh], *to sell,* becomes Vendu [v-on-d-oo]

Rendre [ron-d-ruh], *to return something,* becomes [ron-d-oo]

Mordre [mor-d-ruh], *to bite,* becomes Mordu [mor-d-oo]

Below are some verbs for you to practice forming the *past participle* or *participe passé*.

Visiter [vee-zee-tay] _____

Partir [par-tee-r] _____

Défendre [day-fon-d-ruh] _____

Donner [d-uh-nay] _____

Entendre [on-ton-d-ruh] _____

The Irregular Past Participles

Some verbs have an irregular past participle- that is to say that they do not follow these rules of removing the last two letters and adding the letter stated above. Some verbs have a different letter added. Below are the most common ones.

Faire, *to do* becomes Fait

Lire, *to read* becomes Lu

Pouvoir, *to be able to* become Pu

Prendre, *to take* becomes Pris

Savoir, *to know* becomes Su

Venir, *to come* becomes Venu

Voir, *to see* becomes Vu

Boire, *to drink* becomes Bu

Conduire, *to drive* becomes Conduit

Connaitre, *to know* becomes Connu

Croire, *to believe* becomes Cru

Découvrir, *to discover* becomes Découvert

Dire, *to say* becomes Dit

écrire *to write* becomes écrit

Apprendre, *to learn* becomes Appris

Etre, *to become* été

Avoir, *to have* becomes Eu

These verbs will be ones that you will have to associate with their past participle in your memory and eventually, as you become more familiar with the language, you will notice when you have come across an irregular verb because when you try to create the past participle in the regular way you will feel like it "just doesn't sound right".

Auxiliaries In Passé Composé

We will now put what we have learned about verbs in the past-tense together with the subject we are talking about to form a sentence in the past tense. When it comes to past-tense speaking in French, you must insert a helping verb in between the person you are speaking about (subject) and the action they are doing (to go, to see, to run). Instead of saying, "I ran," in French we say "I have run," "She has run." We use the verb avoir (to have) to help us explain what someone did. In this case, the verb avoir is called the Auxiliary or *L'auxiliaire*. The verb avoir is used its present-tense form, and then the verb we want to say. This form of conjugation is called *passé composé*. In English, this means *composed past,* which essentially is what we are doing- composing a way to explain something that happened in the past. To form the *passé composé* you need the following: the subject + an auxiliary + the past participle.

Below, you can see the present-tense conjugation of the verb avoir, as you learned earlier in the chapter. Memorize this and say it aloud as you will use it quite often when speaking in past-tense.

Avoir As The Auxiliary

J'ai [j-ay]
Tu as [too][ah]
Il a [eel][ah]
Elle a [el][ah]
On a [ohn][ah]
Nous avons [new][ah-v-oh]
Vous avez [v-oo][ah-vay]
Ils ont [eel][oh-nt]
Elles ont [el][oh-nt]

I will now show you some examples of past-tense conjugations of verbs with avoir as the helper verb.

Visiter [vee-zee-tay] becomes Visité [vee-zee-tay]

J'ai visité [j-ay][vee-zee-tay]

Tu as visité [too][ah][vee-zee-tay]

Il a visité [eel][ah][vee-zee-tay]

Elle a visité [el][ah][vee-zee-tay]

On a visité [ohn][ah][vee-zee-tay]

Nous avons visité [new][ah-v-oh][vee-zee-tay]

Vous avez visité [v-oo][ah-vay][vee-zee-tay]

Ils ont visité [eel][oh-nt][vee-zee-tay]

Elles ont visité [el][oh-nt][vee-zee-tay]

Entendre [on-ton-d-ruh] becomes Entendu [on-ton-doo]

J'ai entendu

Tu as entendu

Il a entendu

Elle a entendu

On a entendu

Nous avons entendu

Vous avez entendu

Ils ont entendu

Elles ont entendu

Être As The Auxiliary

There are specific cases where we would use the verb Être as the helper verb (auxiliary) instead of the verb avoir, as we did above. There is no trick to knowing which verbs these are; it is more a matter of memorization. The only thing that could help you is that many of these are verbs that end in -ir. These verbs use Être in its present tense conjugated form as the auxiliary. The conjugation of Être in present tense can be seen below. Memorize this verb conjugation and its pronunciations as you will see this one quite often, as well.

Être conjugated in present tense;
Je suis [j-uh][s-wee], I am
Tu es [too][ay], you are
Il est [eel][ay], he is
Elle est[el][ay], she is
On est [ohn][ay], we are
Nous sommes [n-oo][sum], we are
Vous etes [v-oos][ett-e], you guys are
Ils sont [eel][s-oh-nt], they (masculine) are
Elles sont [el][s-oh-nt], they (feminine) are

I will now give you examples of some of the verbs that always use Être as the auxiliary, conjugated to passé composé, as well as some examples for you to try.

Partir [par-tee-r] becomes Parti [par-tee]

Je suis parti [j-uh][s-wee][par-tee]

Tu es parti [too][ay][par-tee]

Il est parti [eel][ay][par-tee]

Elle est parti [el][ay][par-tee]

On est parti [ohn][ay][par-tee]

Nous sommes [n-oo][sum][par-tee]

Vous etes [v-oos][ett-e][par-tee]

Ils sont [eel][s-oh-nt][par-tee]

Elles sont [el][s-oh-nt][par-tee]

Entrer [on-t-ray] becomes Entré [on-t-ray]

Je suis entré [j-uh][s-wee][on-t-ray]

Tu es entré [too][ay][on-t-ray]

Il est entré [eel][ay][on-t-ray]

Elle est entré [el][ay][on-t-ray]

On est entré [ohn][ay][on-t-ray]

Nous sommes entré [n-oo][sum][on-t-ray]

Vous etes entré [v-oos][ett-e][on-t-ray]

Ils sont entré [eel][s-oh-nt][on-t-ray]

Elles sont entré [el][s-oh-nt][on-t-ray]

The list below indicates all of the irregular verbs in the passé composé, which means they all use the present tense form of etre as their auxiliary.

Devenir *to become* becomes devenu

Revenir *to come back* becomes revenu

Monter *to climb* becomes monté

Rester *to stay* becomes resté

Sortir *to exit* becomes sorti

Passer *to pass* becomes passé

Venir *to come* becomes venu

Aller *to go* becomes allé

Naître *to be born* becomes né

Descendre *to descend* becomes descendu

Entrer *to enter* becomes entré

Rentrer *to re-enter* becomes rentré

Tomber *to fall* becomes tombé

Retourner *to return* becomes retourné

Arriver *to arrive* becomes arrivé

Mourir *to die* becomes mort

Partir *to leave* becomes parti

A fun and easy way to remember these is by remembering the acronym DR. MRS P. VANDERTRAMP, with each letter representing the first letter of one of these irregularly-conjugated verbs.

Future Tense Conjugation

Now that you know how to express yourself in present-tense and past-tense, we will look at how to express yourself in future-tense. After you are comfortable with this, then you will be all set to speak your mind. Watch out world!

When it comes to conjugating verbs into future-tense, it is probably the easiest conjugation you will do in all of the French language. There are endings that are added just like other conjugations, but there are not nearly as many irregular cases in this tense.

-ER and -IR Verbs

For verbs that end in an -er or an -ir, to find the stem is quite easy. We use the form of the verb that you most often see it in when you see a verb on its own. For example;

Aimer, to like *becomes* Aimer
Choisir, to choose *becomes* Choisir

Notice that with the regular verbs in this tense, there is no change to the verb, we will simply add the ending onto this form of the verb. This form of the verb is called The Infinitif or *l'infinitif* [l-an-fee-nee-tee-f].

-RE Verbs

For verbs that end in an -re, we will remove the last *e* from the infinitif form, and then we are all set.

Rendre, to return *becomes* Rendr
Vendre, to sell *becomes* Vendr

Irregular Verbs

Fear not, there are some verbs here that are irregular but not nearly as many as in the passé composé. In this case, we must simply memorize the root that we will use to conjugate the verb to future-tense. An example is below;

Irregular Stems:

Etre, which means "to be" *becomes* Ser-
Aller, to go *becomes* Ir-
Avoir, to have *becomes* Aur-
Courir, to run *becomes* Courr-
Envoyer, to send *becomes* Enverr-

Faire, to do, *becomes* Fer-

Pouvoir, to be able to *become* Pourr-

Savoir, to know *becomes* Saur-

Venir, to come *becomes* Viendr- (this is the same for the similar verbs devenir, to become, tenir, to hold and obtenir, to obtain)

Voir, to se *becomes* Verr

Vouloir, to want *becomes* Voudr-

Changing Stems

Some verbs have changing stems, meaning that the words stay mostly the same except for a change or two. See examples of this below;

Appeler, to call *becomes* Appeller (notice that an extra l was added)

Essayer, to try *becomes* Essaier

Jeter, To dispose of *becomes* Jetter (notice that an extra t was added)

Lever, to lift, to stand *becomes* Lèver

Acheter, to buy *becomes* Achèter

Notice that in these last two examples, an accent was added to the second-to-last *e,* and everything else stays the same.

In all of these irregular forms are like this because it makes for proper or ease of pronunciation in the conjugated form. Because we will add some vowels in the conjugated form, in order to keep pronunciation easy and as least bulky as possible, we add an accent, an extra letter, or even change it entirely in the case of avoir and etre and a few others.

Notice also that the stem always ends with the letter *r*, in all of these cases, and all others in the future tense. This is why we change the verbs that have endings other than the letter *r* like etre and avoir to become ser and aur. If you are trying to conjugate a verb to future tense and you have a stem that you think is correct, but it doesn't end in the letter *r*, try again to find the right stem or check in your notes.

Endings Added In Future Tense

Je/ J'   -ai

Tu -as

Il   -a

Elle -a

On -a

Nous   -ons

Vous   -ez

Ils -ont

Elles   -ont

Notice that the endings we add in the future tense are actually the entire verb avoir conjugated to future tense. This is the same form that we use as an auxiliary in the passé composé form of conjugation, but here we are not using it as an auxiliary, we are using it as the ending that we will put onto the stem. Examples are below. As always, practice your pronunciation;

Etre

Je Serai

Tu Seras

Il/Elle/On Sera

Nous Serons

Vous Serez

Ils/Elles Seront

Avoir

J'Aurai

Tu Auras

Il/Elle/On Aura

Nous Aurons

Vous Aurez

Ils/Elles Auront

Now, study the examples of the conjugations for the future tense of the verbs below.

Aimer

J' aimerai

Tu aimeras

Il/Elle/On aimera

Nous aimerons

Vous aimerez

Ils/Elles aimeront

Jeter

Je jeterai

Tu jeteras

Il/Elle/On jetera

Nous jeterons

Vous jeterez

Ils/Elles jeteront

Faire

Je ferai

Tu feras

Il/Elle/On fera

Nous ferons

Vous ferez

Ils/Elles feront

The regular verb **Jouer**

Je jouerai

Tu joueras

Il/Elle/On jouera

Nous jouerons

Vous jouerez

Ils/Elles joueront

Chapter 4: Numbers

General Number Knowledge

Much like how the alphabet in French is the same one that is used in the English language, the numbers used in French are the same as those used in English as well. Unlike the alphabet, which has some letters that will be pronounced in the same way in English and French respectively, how you say each number is very different between these two languages. In this chapter, we will look at the numbers from one to one hundred and how to pronounce them, as well as other places where you will find numbers such as when speaking about years, money, time, age, and addresses. Each section will include repetition exercises for you complete in order to practice speaking with the correct pronunciation and to get used to the way in which pronunciation can change based on what you are speaking about.

Numbers

In this first section, we will look at the numbers themselves and how to properly pronounce them. Because the numbers look the same, we don't have to go over their meaning and can place all of our focus on how to say what you see and exactly how to pronounce it too. We will begin with the numbers one to ten. Breaking it up into sections will help you to remember each one more clearly. For each set of numbers, practice saying them aloud a few times over before continuing on to the next set of numbers.

One To Ten

1 [uhhn], 2 [duuh], 3 [t-r-wah] (rolled r), 4 [cat-ruh](rolled r), 5 [sank], 6 [see-s], 7 [set], 8 [wee-t], 9 [nuuf], 10 [dee-s]

We will now look at the way each of these numbers is spelled in French. If you are reading, you may come across numbers written instead of just the number itself. The pronunciation is the same, but they are not written phonetically as they are above.

Un, deux, trois, quatre, cinq, six, sept, huit, neuf, dix

One, two, three, four, five, six, seven, eight, nine, ten

Now you can compare the way that each of these numbers is written in French, to the way that each of them is pronounced. You can now also combine this knowledge with your knowledge of the letters of the alphabet from the previous chapter. Notice how the number six is written the exact same way in both languages, but the pronunciation is quite different between the two languages. You can also look for patterns in the way that certain groups of letters placed together changes pronunciation. For example, notice how deux and dix both have the letter *d* at the beginning and the letter *x* at the end, but their pronunciation is completely different. We will now look at the numbers from eleven to nineteen.

Eleven To Nineteen

11 [oh-n-z], 12 [doo-z], 13[t-r-ez](rolled r), 14[cat-or-z], 15[k-an-z], 16[s-ez], 17[dee-set], 18 [dee-sweet], 19 [dee-s-nuf]

These numbers are pronounced quite differently than they are in English, but they do have indications in their pronunciation about which number they are referring to. Compare the numbers one to ten with the numbers eleven to nineteen, and you can see that you will usually find the word for the smaller number somewhere in the word. Below I have written out the French words for each of these numbers where you can see this concept more clearly.

11, 12, 13, 14, 15, 16, 17, 18, 19

Onze, douze, treize, quatorze, quinze, seize, dix-sept, dix-huit, dix-neuf

Onze and *douze* don't follow much of a pattern except that they begin with the same letters as *one* and *two*. Those two you will have to memorize. *Quinze* Is like these two as well in that it must be memorized since it doesn't follow a pattern either. Notice that *treize* begins with the letters *t and r,* which are also the beginning letters of the number 3 which is called *trois* in French. *Quatorze* and *seize* are similar to this as well, beginning with the same letters and sounds as *quatre,* and *six* respectively. Knowing this little trick will give you a clue as to what number is being said if you hear it or see it written, as long as you are familiar with numbers one to ten. The numbers *dix-sept, dix-huit,* and *dix-neuf* are similar to each other in that they all have the number *dix* or ten in them. These are the easiest to figure out as they are literally *ten-*

seven, ten-eight, and *ten-nine* respectively. When hearing someone say or reading any of these numbers from eleven to nineteen, you can try to break the word down into smaller parts in order to determine which number it is. Look for the smaller number (one to ten) inside of the larger number (eleven to nineteen) to help you in your analysis of the number.

Now that you are familiar with the numbers from one to nineteen, we will get into the larger numbers from twenty to one hundred. These numbers will follow a pattern of sorts, and once you learn that, you will be well on your way to saying any number of things you want to say in French! (pun intended).

Twenty to Sixty

20 (Twenty), in French is called *vingt* [v-ain-t].

30 (Thirty), in French is called *trente* [t-ron-t] (with a rolled r)

40 (Forty), in French is called *quarante* [ka-ron-t] (with a rolled r)

50 (Fifty), in French is called *cinquante* [s-ain-k-ont]

60 (Sixty), in French is called *soixante* [s-wah-s-ont]

Get familiar with each of these words on their own, and we will then look at what each set of numbers in between them is called. Say them aloud multiple times until you are comfortable with each one.

Between twenty and sixty-nine, each number in between (such as twenty-one or forty-three) follows the same pattern. We will look at the numbers twenty-one to twenty-nine as an example.

21, *vingt et un*. For any number that is between twenty and sixty-one that has a one at the end, you will say the multiple of ten that it starts with (vingt, trente, quarante, cinquante, or soixante) and then you will say *et un* which in English means *and one*. This is a pretty straight-forward and self-explanatory rule. As long as you know the words and pronunciation for the multiples of ten between twenty and sixty, you can simply add *et un,* and you are ready! The examples of this are below;

21, 31, 41, 51, 61.

Twenty-one, thirty-one, forty-one, fifty-one, sixty-one.

Vingt et un, trente et un, quarante et un, cinquante et un, soixante et un

[v-ain-t][eyy][uhhn], [t-ron-t](with a rolled r)[eyy][uhhn], [ka-ron-t] (with a rolled r)[eyy][uhhn], [s-ain-k-ont][eyy][uhhn], [s-wah-s-ont][eyy][uhhn].

Now that you are comfortable with the above, we will examine the patterns and rules for all of the numbers between twenty and sixty-nine that end with anything other than a zero or a one. These numbers are all quite straight-forward. Begin with the multiple of ten (vingt, trente, quarante, cinquante, or soixante). Then, separated by a hyphen will be the number that comes next. You can see an example of this below using the numbers twenty-two to twenty-nine.

22, *vingt-deux,* 23 *vingt-trois,* 24 *vingt-quatre,* 25 *vingt-cinq,* 26 *vingt-six,* 27 *vingt-sept,* 28 *vingt-huit,* 29 *vingt-neuf.*

If you know the numbers from one to ten and you know the multiples of ten from twenty to sixty, you can form any number in between using this rule. Just substitute either the first or second number or both with the corresponding word, and there you have it. These numbers are quite simple to understand if you hear them spoken or see them written because nothing about the second numbers themselves change, you are simply putting the two numbers together separated by a hyphen. Below are some exercises you can do to test your knowledge of what we have covered so far. While doing these, say the numbers aloud for best results.

Write the corresponding number beside the words below;

Trente-cinq _____   Soixante-huit   _____

Treize _____

Quarante-deux _____   Quarante et un _____

Seize _____

Soixante-six _____   Vingt-trois _____

Onze _____

Vingt-neuf _____   Trente-neuf _____

Dix-neuf _____

Cinquante et un _____ Quarante-quatre _____

Douze _____

Seventy to Ninety-Nine

We will now look at the numbers from seventy to ninety-nine. These ones follow an irregular pattern, so make sure you are comfortable with the above numbers before moving onto this section, especially the numbers between eleven and nineteen. As always, say these numbers aloud as you read them and go over them at least a few times before moving on.

70, Seventy, *Soixante-Dix,* [s-wah-s-ont] [dee-s]

80, Eighty, *Quatre-Vingts,* [cat-ruh](rolled r)[v-ain-t]

90, Ninety, *Quatre-Vingt-Dix,* [cat-ruh](rolled r)[v-ain-t][dee-s]

When we look at these three numbers, their names may seem to be quite confusing. If we break it down, however, we can see that they make quite a bit of sense, and they will actually tell us exactly which number they are referring to.

Seventy, which in French is called *Soixante-Dix,* is the first example we will look at. This number is comprised of two different words: *Soixante* and *Dix.* We know now that *Soixante* means Sixty and that *Dix* means Ten. When we put these together, we can see that it means Sixty plus Ten, which equals Seventy. This rule also applies to the other two numbers, which I will explain for you now.

Quatre-Vingt is comprised of the words *Quatre,* which means Four and *Vingt,* which means Twenty. What this means then is that *Quatre-Vingt* directly translates to mean

Four-Twenty which is exactly what eighty is- four twenties. BEcause 4x20=80, this makes sense.

Quatre-Vingt-Dix, then, is a combination of the last two methods used to determine the meaning. This number includes both a *Dix,* which means Ten and a *Quatre-Vingt,* which means Four Twenties. So, we can combine these to mean Four Twenties plus Ten. 4x20+10=90. This brings us to ninety. The benefit of these last three numbers and even the ones before them is that we can figure out exactly which number we are looking at by breaking the names up into sections and examining them each individually before then bringing them together as a whole.

We will now look at all of the numbers in between Seventy and Seventy-nine. These numbers all follow a similar pattern to each other, which I will now explain. Instead of using the numbers one through nine to describe the last number in a pair such as 78 or 72, we use the numbers eleven through nineteen. This is different from the numbers between twenty-one and sixty-nine which we previously looked at. Those ones use the numbers one through nine to describe the second number in a pair like 43 or 67. I will show you examples of this below.

70, *Soixante-Dix,* [s-wah-s-ont] [dee-s]

Seventy, we have already examined as sixty plus ten. Below are the numbers between seventy-one and seventy-nine.

71, *Soixante-et-onze* [s-wah-s-ont][ayy][oh-n-z]

Seventy-one follows a similar pattern to that of the previous numbers we looked at that finish with the number one where you add the word *and(et)* in between the first and the second number. The difference here, however, is that instead of saying *seventy and one* like we would with the numbers 21, 31, 41, 51 and 61, here we say *Sixty and Eleven*. The reason for this is that the number seventy is said as *Sixty-Ten,* so it would not sound great to say *sixty-ten and one* or *Soixante-Dix et Un*. That's simply too long and too much of a mouthful. So instead, we say *Soixante-et-onze* or *Sixty-and-eleven*. I know this can get confusing, but if you remember that they all make sense if you break them up into smaller parts and that we try to avoid describing a number with too many extra syllables, you will understand them in no time!

72, *Soixante-douze* [s-wah-s-ont][doo-z]
73, *Soixante-treize* [s-wah-s-ont][t-r-ez](rolled r)
74, *Soixante-quatorze* [s-wah-s-ont][cat-or-z]

75, *Soixante-quinze* [s-wah-s-ont][k-an-z]

76, *Soixante-seize* [s-wah-s-ont][s-ez]

77, *Soixante-dix-sept* [s-wah-s-ont][dee-set]

78, *Soixante dix-huit* [s-wah-s-ont][dee-sweet]

79, *Soixante-dix-neuf* [s-wah-s-ont][dee-s-nuf]

Similar to the number Seventy-One or *Soixante-et-onze,* The numbers here also take out the *Dix* or the Ten from the word *Soixante-Dix (70)* and replace it with the numbers after ten (eleven, twelve, thirteen, etc.) This is to avoid a mouthful similarly to above. If you break them up and think about them as Sixty and twelve (72), for example, it makes sense why we name it in this way. The same goes for the numbers between Ninety and Ninety-nine, which we will look at now while this concept is still fresh in your mind.

90, *Quatre-Vingt-Dix,* [cat-ruh](rolled r)[v-ain-t][dee-s]

We saw this number, 90, previously. Remember the reason why we say it this way, as you read below.

91, *Quatre-Vingt Onze* [cat-ruh](rolled r)[v-ain-t][oh-n-z]

With this number, 91, we don't say the *et(and)* because it would just be too many syllables, and by this point, we know what the pattern is and what this number means.

92 *Quatre-Vingt Douze* [cat-ruh](rolled r)[v-ain-t][doo-z]

93 *Quatre-Vingt Treize* [cat-ruh](rolled r)[v-ain-t][t-r-ez](rolled r)

94 *Quatre-Vingt Quatorze* [cat-ruh](rolled r)[v-ain-t][cat-or-z]

95 *Quatre-Vingt Quinze* [cat-ruh](rolled r)[v-ain-t][k-an-z]

96 *Quatre-Vingt Seize* [cat-ruh](rolled r)[v-ain-t][s-ez]

97 *Quatre-Vingt Dix-Sept* [cat-ruh](rolled r)[v-ain-t][dee-set]

98 *Quatre-Vingt Dix-Huit* [cat-ruh](rolled r)[v-ain-t][dee-sweet]

99 *Quatre-Vingt Dix-Neuf* [cat-ruh](rolled r)[v-ain-t][dee-s-nuf]

As with the numbers seventy-one to seventy-nine, we use the number eleven to nineteen to describe the second number in the pair when speaking about the numbers ninety-one to ninety-nine. The meaning can be found in words for these numbers too. I will use Ninety-Three as an example here. *Quatre-Vingt-Treize* or 93 means Four-Twenties and Thirteen. Four twenties is equal to 80, and adding 13 to that gives us 93. While it may seem complicated now, you will be thankful that you can determine all of this just by looking at the number in the future when you are trying to remember all of the French words you have been learning! This applies to all of the numbers between ninety-one and ninety-nine. Practice their pronunciation before moving on.

Now, our final set of numbers before we reach one hundred is the set of numbers between eighty-one and eighty-nine. This group will be quite straight-forward for you at this point. We have seen the number eighty before, along with its pronunciation, but it is written below again to jog your memory. Say it out loud a few times over.

80, *Quatre-Vingts,* [cat-ruh](rolled r)[v-ain-t]

Since the word for eighty literally translates to Four Twenties, if we used the terms between eleven and nineteen to describe these numbers, we would end up in the 90's (and I don't mean the era). This type of nomenclature is also already occupied by all of the numbers between ninety-one and ninety-nine. So, we will keep it simple. For these numbers below, we call them Four Twenties and one, two, three, four, and so on, corresponding to whatever number is second in the pair. For example, the number eighty-one in English (81) is called *Quatre-Vingt Un,* Which means Four twenties plus one, equaling eighty-one. Like I said, this one is quite simple when compared to the seventies and the nineties. All of the examples are laid out for you below along with their pronunciation for you to practice.

81 *Quatre-Vingt* [cat-ruh](rolled r)[v-ain-t][uhhn]

82 *Quatre-Vingt Deux,* [cat-ruh](rolled r)[v-ain-t][duuh]

83 *Quatre-Vingt Trois,* [cat-ruh](rolled r)[v-ain-t][t-r-wah] (rolled r)

84 *Quatre-Vingt Quatre* [cat-ruh](rolled r)[v-ain-t][cat-ruh](rolled r)

85 *Quatre-Vingt Cinq* [cat-ruh](rolled r)[v-ain-t][sank],

86 *Quatre-Vingt Six* [cat-ruh](rolled r)[v-ain-t][see-s]

87 *Quatre-Vingt Sept* [cat-ruh](rolled r)[v-ain-t][set]

88 *Quatre-Vingt Huit* [cat-ruh](rolled r)[v-ain-t] [wee-t]

89 *Quatre-Vingt Neuf* [cat-ruh](rolled r)[v-ain-t][nuuf]

One Hundred

Now we will look at the number one hundred and all of the numbers in between one hundred and one thousand. This will follow essentially the same rules as the numbers between one and one hundred, but with a few small differences.

100, One Hundred, *Cent* [s-on-t]

For the numbers between one hundred and one hundred ninety-nine, you will follow all of the same rules as you just learned for the numbers between one and one hundred, except they will all have the word *Cent* at the beginning. Some examples are below.

Cent un = 101

Cent Vingt Cinq = 125

Cent Trente Six =136

Cent Soixante et Un =161

Cent Soixante-Dix = 170

Cent Quatre-Vingt = 180

Cent Quatre-Vingt Un = 181

Cent Quatre-Vingt Dix-Neuf = 199

Cent Quatre-Vingt Treize = 193

Cent Soixante Quatorze = 174

This is the same for the numbers between two hundred and one and two hundred ninety-nine, and so on until nine hundred ninety-nine. Below are the words for the multiples of one hundred. For all of the numbers in between, follow the same rules laid out earlier in this chapter.

200, *Deux Cent*

300, *Trois Cent*

400, *Quatre Cent*

500, *Cinq Cent*

600, *Six Cent*

700, *Sept Cent*

800, *Huit Cent*

900, *Neuf Cent*

One Thousand And Beyond

Before we move on to looking at practical uses for these numbers, we will now look at the Numbers beyond one hundred.

1000, One Thousand, *Un Mille* [uhn][m-eel]

The number one thousand, or *Un Mille* can be said at the beginning of a group of numbers with at least 4 digits to make it one million-something. Examples of this are below.

1001 *Mille et Un*

1350 *Mille Trois Cent Cinquante*

1270 *Mille Deux Cent Soixante-Dix*

1593 *Mille Cinq Cent Quatre-Vingt Treize*

1120 *Mille Cent Vingt*

As you can see above, the rules for every number after the One in one thousand, remain the same. These rules for all of the multiples of ten and the words we use to describe the multiples of one hundred remain the same. As long as you know these, the only thing left to learn is the names for the multiples of one thousand.

One thousand, *Mille*
Two thousand, *Deux Mille*
Three thousand, *Trois Mille*
Four thousand, *Quatre Mille*
Five thousand, *Cinq Mille*
Six thousand, *Six Mille*
Seven thousand, *Sept Mille*
Eight thousand, *Huit Mille*
Nine thousand, *Neuf Mille*
Ten thousand, *Dix Mille*

As you can see above, the only difference when talking in the thousands is adding the word *Mille* after the number of thousands about which you are talking. After ten thousand, you keep going up in the regular sequence of numbers that we have already learned until you reach 999 999, or nine hundred ninety-nine thousand nine hundred and ninety-nine. This number is called *Neuf Cent Quatre Vingt Dix-Neuf*

Mille (nine hundred ninety-nine thousand) *Neuf Cent* (nine hundred) *Quatre-Vingt Dix-Neuf* (ninety-nine). From this example, you can tell that the only thing different here is that there are two groups of hundreds placed together, and where you would say *thousand* in English, you say *mille* instead.

One Million

One million is the next number we come to, and similarly to one thousand, once you know the words for all of the millions from one to nine hundred ninety-nine, you can figure out how to say any number in between as they all follow the same pattern as those between one and one hundred.

One Million, *Un Million* [uhn][mee-lee-yon]

To figure out how to say any of the other millions, just substitute the number, such as thirty in for the *un*(one) like so,

30 000 000, Thirty million, *Trente Million*.

After millions come billions and trillions. These next two you will likely never use, but I have included them just for interest's sake. They are a little bit confusing, but give their pronunciation a try and then move onto the next section.

One Billion, *Un Milliard,* [uhn][meel-yard]

One Trillion, *Un Billion,* [uhn][beel-yon]

Now that you know how to say every number under the sun, we are going to look at some practical examples of when and how to use them. It is rare for people to use numbers in conversation without having some sort of context. Below, we will explore their most common uses.

Date (day, year, months)

We will now look at how to say the date in French. It is a little different from the way that we do this in English in terms of the order of the words. Read below to find out how we do this.

Years

We will now look at the way that we say years in French. While it may be a little confusing if you are not too familiar with the way to say large numbers in French. In this section, I will teach you the main things you need to know when it comes to years so that you will be able to understand other people talking about years, reading things about years, and when you yourself want to mention a year in conversation.

The Word For Year

There are two words we use to say a year. Which word you use will depend on the number which the year ends with. For all years that end with the number zero (0), you will use the word l'an [l-o-n]. This means *"the year."* For years ending in any number other than zero, you will use the term *l'année* [l-ah-nay], which also means *"the year."* If you forget and mix up which of these to use with which years, don't fret, nobody will curse you for using the wrong form of the words *the year*. It is, however, good to know both forms so that if you hear them you know what the person is saying.

L'année, the year
L'an, the year

In conversation, we will often be talking about the year in which something happened, the year in which we will be doing something in the future, or the year in which we were born. Therefore, the most common years we would be using would be in the 1800's, 1900's and the 2000's. We will look at how you would say this group of years below.

The word *Mille* means one thousand. You will use this in almost any year you are talking about. If you are talking about the future or present years, you will then say *Deux Mille,* which, as you now know means "two thousand" (deux, as you learned earlier in this chapter means two). The next most common numbers will be 900, which in French is *neuf cent* and 800 which in French is *huit cent,* which you also know already now as you learned the names for 8 and 9 earlier. *Cent* means hundred.

Mille, thousand
Cent, hundred

Now you know how to say the following years;

1000, mille
2000, deux mille
1800, mille huit cent
1900, mille neuf cent
2800 deux mille huit cent
2900 deux mille neuf cent

(These last two you wouldn't use too often, but they are numbers you could say now nonetheless)

The next thing you will need to know is the multiples of 10 from 20 to 90. These are below, along with their pronunciations. Practice these ones as well before moving onto the next section, where we will put all of your knowledge together.

20 (Twenty), in French is called vingt [v-ain-t].

30 (Thirty), in French is called trente [t-ron-t] (with a rolled r)

40 (Forty), in French is called quarante [ka-ron-t] (with a rolled r)

50 (Fifty), in French is called cinquante [s-ain-k-ont]

60 (Sixty), in French is called soixante [s-wah-s-ont]

70, Seventy, in French is called Soixante-Dix, [s-wah-s-ont] [dee-s]

80, Eighty, in French is called Quatre-Vingts, [cat-ruh](rolled r)[v-ain-t]

90, Ninety, in French is called Quatre-Vingt-Dix, [cat-ruh](rolled r)[v-ain-t][dee-s]

You now also know how to say all of the following years and more;

1990 Mille neuf cent quatre-vingt dix
2020 Deux mille vingt
2030 Deux mille trente

Now, remember how earlier in this chapter, you learned how to say the numbers from 1 to 10 and from 11 to 19. These will then help you to finish off the years and can help you to say almost any year you will need! These numbers are below to refresh your memory in case you need them.

1, Un,

2, deux,

3, trois,

4, quatre,

5, cinq,

6, six,

7, sept,

8, huit,

9, neuf,

10, dix

11 onze

12 douze

13 treize

14 quatorze

15 quinze

16 seize

17 dix-sept

18 dix-huit

19 dix-neuf

And now, you know how to say all of the following years as well as many more;

2019 Deux mille dix-neuf
1880 Mille huit cent quatre-vingts
1902 Mille neuf cent deux
2001 Deux mille un
2010 Deux mille Dix
1965 Mille Neuf Cent soixante cinq

As a final note, when it comes to talking about years, there are two more words that we sometimes use when speaking about years. Those are the years A.D. And the years B.C. In French we say *ap.JC* and *av.JC*, respectively. These shorthands refer to the eras "Before Jesus Christ" and "After Jesus Christ." In French we say *apres Jesus-Christ* and *avant Jesus-Christ*. The pronunciation for these is below;

Apres, [ah-pray]
Avant [ah-vont]
Jesus-Christ, [j-ay-z-oo][k-r-ee](rolled r)

In practice, it would look like this;

Days Of The Week

In this section, we will learn the days of the week and how to use them in a sentence. First, practice reading the days of the week aloud along with their pronunciation a few times over to get comfortable with them all.

Lundi [l-uh-n-dee], Monday
Mardi [mah-r-dee](rolled r), Tuesday
Mercredi [meh-k-re-dee](rolled r), Wednesday
Jeudi [j-uh-dee], Thursday
Vendredi [von-d-ruh-dee] (rolled r), Friday
Samedi [sah-m-dee], Saturday
Dimanche [dee-mon-sh], Sunday

When we use the days of the week in a sentence, we do not capitalize them in French. This is unlike English where we would capitalize the days of the week as they are considered names or titles. If you see it written and are wondering if the newspaper printing company made a mistake, it is not a mistake, just the French way!

Un Jour, a day
La Semaine, The week

Les jours de la semaine, the days of the week

Prochaine, next

Dernière, last

Chaque jour, every day

Hier, yesterday

Demain, tomorrow

Aujourd'hui, today

We will look at some example sentences for you to practice now;

Quel jour est-ce qu'on voit le film? What day do we see the movie?

J'ai travaillé 3 jours la semaine dernière. I worked 3 days last week.

C'est la fête d'anniversaire de mon fils le mardi prochaine. It's my son's birthday party next Tuesday.

Il fait du ski chaque jour sauf lundi. He skis every day except Monday.

Le jour du semaine que j'aime le plus c'est vendredi. The day of the week that I like the most is Friday.

Months Of The Year

Les mois, months

Un année, a year

Un an, a year

Les mois de l'année, the months of the year

In this chapter, we will look at the months of the year. These, similar to the days of the week, are not capitalized when we write them in a sentence. This is different from English as we would always capitalize names and titles like this.

January *le Janvier,* [luh][j-on-vee-ay]

February *le février,* [luh][fay-v-ree-ay]

March *le mars* [luh][mah-r-se]

April *l'avril,* [l-ah-v-ree-l]

May *le mai,* [luh][may]

June *le juin,* [luh][j-wah-n]

July *le juillet* [luh][j-wee-ay]

August *le août* [luh][oot]

September *le septembre,* [luh][sep-tom-b-ruh]

October, *l'octobre,* [l-oct-oh-b-ruh]

November, *le novembre,* [luh][no-vom-b-ruh]

December, *le décembre,* [luh][day-som-b-ruh]

Practice saying the names of the months aloud a few times over so you get comfortable with the pronunciation, and then we will look at them used in sentences below.

Mon anniversaire est dans le mois de juin. My birthday is in the month of June.

Ma fille an ete née le 30 janvier. My daughter was born January 30th.

Les mois entres novembre et mars sont très froid à l'état de New York. The months between November and March are very cold in the state of New York.

Il pleut beaucoup dans le mois d'avril. It rains a lot in the month of April.

Dates

Dates are the next logical step when you know how to talk about years and months. We will put that knowledge together in this section so that you are able to talk about dates with their years. When talking about a date, we will begin by saying *le,* which means "the." This is similar to English as it looks like this;

Je suis nee le, I was born the...
Il est nee le, he was born the...
Tu es nee le, you were born the...

Le 6 janvier 1920, The sixth of January, 1920

In French we write the dates in the order shown above, with the number first followed by the month and then the year, whereas in English we would say January 6th, 1920.

Time

The first thing we will look at in this section is time. In French, there are different names than in English for things like seconds, minutes and hours. You will also need to have some understanding of numbers from 1 to 12 and how to say things like half an hour or 45 minutes. We will look at all this and more in this first section on time.

The following list demonstrates the words in French for the sections of time that we use like seconds and hours. Take some time to go over this and to practice your pronunciation.

Une Seconde [seh-k-on-d], second
Une Minute [mee-n-oo-t], minute
Une Heure [euh-ruh], hour
Un Jour[j-oo-r], day
Une Semaine [suh-m-en], week
Un Mois [m-wah], month
Une Anee [ah-nay], year
Un Dizaine d'annees [dee-z-en][d-ah-nay], ten years/ tens of years

Une vingtaine d'annees [van-ten][d-ah-nay], twenty years

When we talk about "the time" as we say in English, we would normally say something like "what time is it?" or "what's the time." In French, we say *L'Heure [l-euh-ruh]*, Which is the equivalent of "the time" in French. You may also see it written as *heure* which is essentially "time" or "hour." Below, you can see how we would use this in a phrase or in a conversation.

C'est quoi l'heure? What's the time?

Quelle heure a-til?, What time is it?

À Quelle heure est-ce-qu'on quitte?, What time are we leaving at?

À Quelle heure avez-vous ete née?, What time were you born at?

L'École commence à quelle heure?, What time does school start at?

Now, we will learn the numbers from 1 to 12, as we will use these when talking about time. First, we will learn the way that the hours are said in French, before moving on to more specific times.

1:00	*Une heure*
2:00	*Deux heures*
3:00	trois *heures*
4:00	quatre *heures*
5:00	cinq *heures*
6:00	six *heures*
7:00	sept *heures*
8:00	huit *heures*
9:00	neuf *heures*
10:00	dix *heures*
11:00	onze *heures*
12:00	douze *heures*

When we talk about hours in French, it is quite straight-forward, as we say the number and then the word "hours." Douze heures, for example, literally translates to mean "twelve hours." There isn't really a word for "o'clock" like we have in English.

We will now look at how we say things like fifteen minutes or half an hour in French. This will involve a bit more number knowledge, but with practice, you will be using it seamlessly in no time.

_:15	*Quinze*

_:30   *Trente*

_:45   *Quarante Cinq*

When it comes to things like "a quarter past twelve," we would say this in French as well, but in the following ways;

_:30, et demi

3:15, three fifteen, quarter past three, *trois heures quinze, trois heures et quart*

3:30, three thirty, *trois heures trente, trois heures et demi*

3:45, three forty-five, quarter to four, *trois heures quarante-cinq, quatre heures moins quart*

Now that you know these, you can say virtually any time that you see on the clock by substituting the hour and whichever of the three options above you need. These three options, along with all of the hours themselves will give you enough information to understand and say almost any time without having to know how to say all of the numbers from one to sixty in French. Below are a few more terms concerning time that will help you, as well.

In French, the 24-hour clock is used instead of the 12-hour clock that we use in North America. You can use either or when speaking, and people will usually know what you mean, as long as you specify if it is AM or PM, which you are talking about. It will, however, be helpful to know the numbers from 13 to 24 as well since a person speaking to you will likely use the 24-hour format when talking about time.

Avant-Midi, AM
Apres-Midi, PM
Midi, Noon

1:00PM, une heure de l'après- midi
11:00 AM onze heure de le matin

While the correct term for AM is *avant-midi,* when we use this in conversation, we would say *de le matin* instead, which translates to "in the morning." The reason for this is that Avant-midi translates to mean "before noon" and apres-midi translates to mean "after noon." Therefore, another way to say AM is "in the morning."

13:00 treize heures
14:00 quatorze heures
15:00 quinze heures
16:00 seize heures
17:00 dix-sept heures
18:00 dix-huit heures

19:00 dix-neuf heures

20:00 vingt heures

21:00 vingt et un heures

22:00 vingt deux heures

23:00 vingt trois heures

24:00 vingt quatre heures

We will look at some sentence examples now so you can see how to use these times practically by answering the questions that we learned earlier in this section.

Question: *C'est quoi l'heure? What's the time?*

Answer: *C'est dix-heures dans le matin. It's 10 o'clock in the morning.*

Question: *Quelle heure a-til?, What time is it?*

Answer: *Il est vingt-trois heures. It is 23:00 (11:00PM).*

Question: *À Quelle heure est-ce-que vous quittez?, What time are you leaving at?*

Answer: *On quitte dans trois heures, à cinq heures de l'après-midi. We are leaving in three hours, at 5 o'clock in the afternoon (5:00PM).*

Question: *À Quelle heure avez-vous ete née?, What time were you born at?*

Answer: *Je suis née à six-heures et demi du matin. I was born at 6:30 in the morning.*

Question: *L'École, il commence à quelle heure?, School, what time does school start at?*

Answer: *L'école, il commence à neuf heures moins quart dans le matin. School starts at a quarter to nine in the morning (8:45AM).*

Answer 2: *L'école commence à huit heures quarante-cinq dans le matin. School starts at eight forty-five in the morning.*

Chapter 5: Seasons

The seasons are often included when talking about dates and months, so we will now look at these, which you can add to the dates above to describe the time of year or the day in enough detail.

Le Printemps, Spring
L'ete, Summer
L'automne, Fall/ Autumn
L'hiver, Winter

Sentence Examples

We will now look at some sentences that will put all of the knowledge you have gained in the last two chapters together into one sentence.

Le printemps est ma saison préférée. Spring is my favorite season

Le Noël se passe dans l'hiver. Christmas happens in the winter

Je suis née dans le printemps, sur mardi le trois mai, mille neuf cent quatre-vingt à dix heures du matin. I was born in the spring on Wednesday, May 3rd, 1980, at 10 o'clock in the morning.

Chapter 6: Colors

In this chapter, we will talk about colors and how we will use them in practice. As we discussed earlier in this book, colors are masculine nouns. Therefore, they will be paired with the words *le, de* etcetera. However, the word color itself in French is a feminine noun. *La couleur* means the color. For example, you would say *la couleur est le bleu* (the color is blue). In this sentence, you can see that color is a feminine word, and the word blue is masculine.

Below, you will see the most common colors and their French names. Keep in mind that all of these colors are masculine nouns.

Yellow, jaune

Black, noir/noire

Blue, bleu/bleue

Purple, violet/violette

Green, vert/verte

Orange, orange

White, blanc/blanche

Gray, gris/grise

Brown, brun

Red, rouge

Pink, rose

In a sentence, colors are often used as adjectives, meaning that they describe nouns. This means that we must adjust the ending of the color as an adjective which agrees with the gender of the noun it is talking about. This is the same for a plural noun. It must agree with the plurality of the noun by having an *s* added to the end of the word. You can see this below;

La robe blanche, *the white dress* [blanche used because robe is feminine]

Les souliers jaunes, *the yellow shoes* [an s added to jaune because souliers is plural]

The exception to this is that colors that already end with the letter e will not have another e added when it is paired with a feminine noun. This would be too much of a mouthful to say, especially in a sentence.

Sentence Examples

Elle porte une jupe verte, *she is wearing a green skirt.*

Il a mangé un sandwich sur du pain blanc. *He ate a sandwich on white bread.*

Nous aimons la couleur rouge. *We like the color red.*

Chapter 7: Food And Drinks

Groceries

In this chapter, we will look at everything related to food. We will look at how to go through the entire process in a restaurant from walking in, to leaving, including ordering food and asking for anything you may need. We will look at some common foods and how to say them in French, as well as things like grocery shopping and fast food. At the end of each food section located within this chapter, you will find sentence examples for how you can use these words in a sentence. This will also show you what other words are commonly used in conjunction with common food words. At

122

the end of the chapter is a vocabulary list where you can find all of the pronunciations for the words in this chapter.

First, though, we will look at the words we use for food itself.

La nourriture, food
Manger, to eat
Un repas, a meal
Avoir Faim, to be hungry
La cuisine, the kitchen

Le Petit Dejeuner, Breakfast
Le dejeuner, lunch
Le diner, Dinner
Diner, to have dinner
Le gouter, snack
Gouter, to taste
Bon Appetit, enjoy your food/ let's eat

Groceries

When it comes to groceries, you may need to know how to ask for things when you go to the store. You may also need to know what the most common foods are called in French for conversation sake. Here in this section, we will look at these.

Staples

Staples are those things that we keep in the house all the time, and that comes in handy no matter what we are making. Below, you will find these along with their names in French.

Les oeufs, eggs

Le pain, bread

Le beurre, butter

Du lait, milk

La farine, flour

L'huile d'olive, olive oil

Le sucre, sugar

Le fromage, cheese

J'aime manger le fromage avant- le dîner, I like eating cheese before dinner.

Les Oeufs sur le pain est mon petit déjeuner préféré. Eggs on toast is my favourite breakfast.

Je mis du sucre dans mon Café. I put sugar in my coffee.

Vegetables And Fruits

Now we will look at the names for the most common vegetables and fruits in French. Their pronunciation can be found in the vocabulary list at the end of the chapter.

Les legumes, vegetables

Les asperges, asparagus

La carotte, a carrot

Les champignon, mushrooms

Le concombre, a cucumber

La laitue, lettuce

Un oignon, an onion

La pomme de terre, a potato

Le mais, corn

La tomate, a tomato

Les epinards, spinach

Les fruits, fruits

Un ananas, a pineapple

Une banane, a banana

Une fraise, a strawberry

Les cerises, cherries

Une orange, an orange

Une pomme, an apple

Un raisin, a grape

J'adore les légumes vert comme le concombre, les asperges et la laitue. I love green vegetables like cucumbers, asparagus and lettuce.

Je ne sais pas si une tomate est un fruit ou un vegetale. I don't know if a tomato is a fruit or a vegetable.

Les raisins forment le vin après quelques processus. Grapes form wine after some processes.

Meat

The words in this section describe foods related to or containing meat.

Le viande, meat

Le poulet, chicken

La dinde, turkey

De boeuf, beef

Le jambon, ham

Le bifteck, steak

Le poisson, fish

Le porc, pork

Le saucisson, sausage

Les ailes de poulet: Chicken wings

Le blanc de poulet: Chicken breast

Le consommé du volaille: Chicken broth

Le coquelet: Young male chicken

La poulard: Young female chicken

Le poulet/poule: Chicken

Le poulet rôti: Roast chicken

La volaille: White meat

La cuisse: Dark meat

Les végétariens ne mangent pas le viande.

Les végétaliens ne mangent pas ni le poisson, ni le fromage, ni le viande, ni les oeufs, ni du lait. *Vegans don't eat fish or cheese or meat or eggs or milk.*

J'aime manger le poulet mais seulement la volaille et pas la cuisse. I like eating chicken but only the white meat and not the dark meat.

Others/ Dishes

Les pâtes, pasta

Le riz, rice

Le chocolat, chocolate

Le gateau, cake

La tarte, pie

La confiture, jam

La confiture sur du pain est une bonne casse-croûte. Jam on bread is a good snack.

On mange le gâteau chaque fois qu'on a une fête d'anniversaire. We eat cake every time we have a birthday party.

Qu'est-ce que tu aime le plus, les pâtes ou le riz? Which do you like better, pasta or rice?

Fast-Food

In French, fast food is called *Le restauration rapide*. This means exactly the same as in English. The most common fast food words are found in this section.

Les frites, French fries
Un Hamburger, a hamburger
Le hot dog
La boisson non-alcoolisée, a pop
La pizza, pizza
La garniture, the filling
Les beignets de poulet, chicken nuggets
Le poulet frit, fried chicken
Le poisson avec des frites, fish and chips
Le soda, soda pop
La sauce, sauce
À emporter, to take-out
Le plateau, a tray
La paille, a straw

Le poulet frit avec de la sauce piquante s'il vous plaît. Fried chicken with hot sauce please.

J'ai oublié une paille pour mon soda! I forgot a straw for my soda!

Je voudrais un hamburger avec du fromage et du laitue. I would like a hamburger with cheese and lettuce.

Restaurant

We will now look at the process of ordering food from a restaurant, as it is slightly different in French than in English. After reading through this section and practicing it a few times, you will be all set to begin visiting French restaurants, and any other restaurant in French-speaking places! To begin, we will look at the names of the meals themselves that you may need to know when you are reading a menu. First, though, if you want to reserve a table at a restaurant, you can do so by calling on the phone in most cases. The conversation would look something like this;

-Bonjour, Restaurant _____ C'est Pierre.
-Bonjour, je voudrais réserver un table s'il vous plaît.
- Pour combien de personnes?
- Pour deux personnes
-Pour quand?

- Pour demain soir à dix-huit heure

- A quel nom?

- Giroux.

-Daccord, a demain Monsieur Giroux!

-Merci, beaucoup

The translation for this phone dialogue is below;

"Hello, _____ Restaurant, Pierre Speaking."

"Hello, I would like to reserve a table, please."

"For how many people?"

"For two people."

"For when?"

"For tomorrow night at 18:00"

"Under what name?"

"Giroux"

"Right, see you tomorrow, Mr. Giroux!"

"Thank you very much."

Then, when you arrive at the restaurant, in order to find your reservation you will say;

-Bonjour, vous avez une réservation?

- Bonjour, oui. J'ai réservé une table pour deux personnes au nom de Giroux.

- Bon, suivez-moi

The translation for this in-person dialogue is below;

"Hello, do you have a reservation?"

"Hello, yes. I reserved a table for two people under the name Giroux."

"Great, follow me."

Un restaurant, a restaurant

*Le menu, **the** menu*

*Un menu, **a** menu*

L'entrée/ L'hors d'oeuvre, the appetizer

Le plat principal, the main course

Le dessert, dessert

À la carte, from the menu

Prix fixe, Set menu

Le fromage — Cheese plate

Le digestif — After-dinner drink

When you enter the restaurant, if you are supposed to seat yourself, there will likely be a sign saying *Asseyez-vous memes*, which means seat yourselves. If you don't see this, someone will likely seat you. If you are just checking out a restaurant to see if you'd like to eat there, you can ask for a menu when you enter by saying *Bonjour, La carte, s'il vous plaît*, which means, "hello, the menu please." Once you are seated, you may need to ask for some extra things or for some clarification regarding the menu. This section will walk you through all of these possible things.

This first section deals with the words you may need to know when ordering your food;

Je voudrais: I would like...

Plat Du jour: Special/ Dish Of the day

Le serveur: the waiter

La serveuse: the waitress

Compris/Inclus: Included

Végétarien: Vegetarian

Végétalien: Vegan

Bien cuit: Well done

Un morceau: A piece

À point: Medium rare

Bleu, saignant: Rare ("blue"/ "bleeding")

Provençal: Cooked with tomatoes, anchovies, and olives

À votre goût: To your liking

Fumé: Smoked

Frit(e): Fried

À la vapeur: Steamed

Un méli-mélo: An assortment

Haché: Ground (meat)

Piquant: Spicy

Rôti: Roasted

This section now will look at things you may need once you receive your food, or while you are eating.

La Biere, beer
Le vin, wine
Le sel [luh][s-el], The salt
Le poivre [luh][p-wah-v-ruh], The pepper
Des serviettes [day][s-air-vee-et-s], Napkins
De l'eau [duh][l-oh], Some water
Du cafe [doo][kah-fay], Some coffee
Du The [doo][tay], Some tea
Le ketchup [luh]ketchup, The Ketchup
Le sauce piquante [luh][soh-s][pee-k-ont], The hot sauce
Allergique à: Allergic to
L'assiette: Plate
Délicieux: Delicious
Une tranche: A slice

You can ask for any one of the above items by saying the word, followed by *s'il vous plaît* [seel][voo][p-l-ay], which means, please.

One thing to note is that the word *Garçon*, which means "boy" or *Fille*, which means "girl." You may have heard this being used in the movies when a restaurant scene comes on. However, this is considered very rude in French. What you should say in order to get the attention of the waiter is to say *Excusez-moi monsieur* or *Excusez-moi madame.*

When you finish eating, they may come around and offer to take your plate. If this is the case, you can say *C'est termine,* which means "It's finished" or "The plate is finished."

and you are ready for your bill you can say *L'addition, s'il vous plaît.* L'addition is *the bill* or *the check.* In a French restaurant, you will need to ask for the cheque when you are ready for it as they will prefer not to make you feel like you are being asked to leave. So, when you are ready, you can use this phrase to ask for it.

L'addition, the bill
Le pourboire, the tip

After they bring you anything, or when you are leaving, and you want to thank them, you will say;

Merci [meh-r-see], Thank you

Merci beaucoup [meh-r-see][b-oh-k-oo], Thanks a lot, thank you so much

Merci bien [meh-r-see][bee-yen], Thank you very much

If you want to be more formal when you say thank you, you can say "thank you, sir" or "thank you, ma'am." You can also combine any of the above ways of saying thank you with sir or ma'am to be extra polite for example;

Merci Monsieur [meh-r-see][moh-see-uh-r], Thank you Sir

Merci Madame [meh-r-see][mah-dah-m], Thank you ma'am

Merci Beaucoup Madame [meh-r-see][b-oh-k-oo][mah-dah-m], Thank you so much ma'am.

Try an exercise now to practice this;

You just walked into a restaurant, and you see is a sign saying, "Asseyez-vous memes." You then walk into the dining room and seat yourself at a small round table. When you see a waiter walk by, you catch her eye because you want to ask her for the menu. When she stops at your table, you say _____. After you have looked at the menu, you decide that you want to order a coffee. When the waitress comes by you again you say _____.

Then, after drinking your coffee, you decide that you need some Sugar (*du sucre* [soo-k-ruh]) so you say _____. Once you finish your coffee, you are ready for your bill. You call the waitress over by saying _____. You then ask her for the bill by saying _____. Then, you pay your bill, and you are ready to leave. As you are walking out the door, you say _____.

Coffee Shop

When it comes to a coffee shop, you will order in a similar way, but the things you will order will be different. These will be the following;

Un cafe, a coffee

Un café au lait, a latte

Un café décaféiné, a decaffeinated coffee

Un café noisette, a hazelnut coffee

Un café américain, an americano

café filtré, a filter coffee

Un café glacé, an iced coffee

Du thé, tea

Un thé glacé, iced tea

Un thé vert, green tea

Un thé noir, black tea

Chocolat chaud, hot chocolate

Du lait s'il vous plaît, some milk please

Du Sucre s'il vous plaît, some sugar please

Now, in either a restaurant or a coffee shop, there are slightly different ways to go about ordering. First, you will say either

Je voudrais, I would like

or

Je prendrai, I will take

If you are not ready to order yet and you need another minute, you will say

Je n'ai pas encore choisi, I haven't chosen yet.

Or

Une minute encore s'il vous plaît

We will look at some examples for either a restaurant or a coffee shop below.

Je prendrai un bifteck bien cuit s'il vous plaît. I will take a steak well done, please

Je voudrais un chocolat chaud s'il vous plaît. I would like a hot chocolate, please

On prendrait deux cafés, américaines s'il vous plaît. We will take two filter coffees, please.

Nous voudrions trois tasses de bière s'il vous plaît. We would like three glasses of beer, please.

Chapter 8: Meeting And Greeting

When it comes to meeting people or running into people on the street, there are some common things you will say as a formality. We will look at these below.

Phrases You Need To Know

If you need to ask someone how to say a certain thing in French, you can ask them, Comment dit-on ... en francais? And then insert the thing that you are asking them about. For example, you can ask them, "comment dit-on banana en francais? [coh-mon][dee-t][ohn]banana[oh-n][f-ron-say], how do you say banana in French.

In French, if we want to say see you later, we would say *à toute à l'heure* [ah][too-t][ah][l-err]. If you want to say see you later, on a specific day, we would say, for example, "see you Tuesday," à mardi! [ah][mah-r-dee].

If you want to ask someone for help for anything you can say

"Est-ce que vous pouvez m'aider?" [ess-kuh][voo][poo-vay][m-eh-day] which means "Can you help me?"

If a person asks a question but you are unsure of the answer, you can say "Je ne sais pas" [j-uh][nuh][say][pah] which means "I don't know."

If you want to ask someone about something, what something is, or if you need clarification about something specific you can say "Qu'est-ce que c'est?" [k-ess][kuh]say], this means "What is it?" Or It can also mean what is _____. You then will insert whatever you are wondering about such as

Qu'est-ce que c'est ca? "Which means what is that?"

Qu'est-ce que c'est (insert word in French that you aren't sure of the meaning of), this could be something like Qu'est-ce que c'est *l'hiver?* Say this if you aren't sure what they said. Then, they will tell you that *l'hiver* means *winter.*

Répétez, s'il vous plaît or Répète s'il vous plaît, *Can you repeat that please?*

This is a way of asking someone to repeat themselves. If you want to directly ask them to repeat themselves instead of just saying "sorry?" you can ask them this. As we learned earlier, using vous is a polite way, and using tu is a less formal way that you would use with friends.

Plus lentement [p-loo][lon-tuh-mon-t], *slower*. You can use this phrase to ask someone to speak slower for you if you are having trouble understanding them because of a different accent than you are used to or if they are speaking too fast for you to understand. Plus, lentement directly translates to "more slowly." If you want to make it even more polite you can say s'il vous plait at the end of this phrase and form it as a question.

Encore Une fois [on-k-or][oo-n][f-wah], *one more time*. This can be used similarly to the above phrase, but this one is used to ask someone to repeat themselves in a different way. This way doesn't mean that you want them to speak slower, it's more for when you just simply did not hear someone. If you want them to repeat themselves but in a slower voice, be sure to use the previous phrase instead. This one can be used if you are in a loud place and cannot hear someone or if they mumbled their words. Someone may say this phrase to you if they are having some trouble understanding your accent but not to worry, just press on and repeat yourself.

Greetings

Common greetings that you will use in French when you first meet someone or when you encounter someone and begin a conversation. This will help you to know how to get a conversation started. All of the words italicized within the text here can be found in a vocabulary list at the end of the chapter. If you want to practice pronunciations of any phrase before you continue, flip to the end of the chapter before coming back to continue reading here.

The first word we will begin with is how to say hello or hi. This you will use quite often, so spend some time practicing this word and its pronunciation. In French, hello is *Bonjour* [bon-j-oor].

Another one that is similar to hello that you may use often is *Bonsoir* [b-ohn-s-wah], which means "good evening." This one can be used both formally and informally, depending on the circumstances.

There are a few other ways to say hello, some that are less formal and are more of a casual way to greet someone that is usually reserved only for your friends or family members. They are as follows;

Salut [sah-loo], which can mean either hello or goodbye and is quite informal, like saying "hey" and "see ya," but with a single word that can be used anytime.

Coucou [k-oo-k-oo] this one is a silly greeting that means "hey!" for close friends and people like your siblings.

Allô [ah-loh], which is usually used when you pick up a phone call or when you call someone. This is primarily used in Canadian French; it is a sort of combination of both English and French in one.

If you are meeting someone for the first time and you want to introduce yourself, you would say *Je m'appelle* [j-uh][m-ah-p-el]. This directly translates to mean, "I am called." You would say *Je m'appelle* _____ (insert your name).

To introduce someone else, like if you bring a friend to a party or something of the sort, you would say *Je te présente* _____ (insert their name) [j-uh][tuh][pr-eh-s-on-tuh]. If you want to say this more formally like if you are introducing someone in a work-related meeting, you would say *Je vous présente* _____ (insert their name) [j-uh][v-oo][pr-eh-s-on-tuh].

When asking someone their name, you would say one of two things. Remember how, in the introduction to this book, I introduced the concept of addressing someone using different words depending on if they are your friend or if they are an acquaintance to whom you want to show respect? This is where that concept will come to life, and I will show you the different options and examples of this. Firstly, if you are speaking to a friend or someone who is deemed an equal of yours, you would say *Comment t'appelles-tu?* [k-ohm-on][t-app-el][too]. *Tu* is a less formal and more casual way of addressing a person. If however, you want to show them respect or if they are an elder or something like this, you would say *Comment vous appelez-vous?* [k-ohm-on][v-oo-z][app-el-ay][v-oo]. In English, we would ask "what is your name?" or "...and you are?" or something along those lines, regardless of who we are asking, but in French this distinction is important.

After you have introduced yourself to someone and you have exchanged names, either you or the other person will say, *enchanté* [on-sh-on-tay], which is how we say, "Nice to meet you," or it is a pleasure to meet you. It directly translates to mean "Enchanted to meet you."

There are also a couple of other options that are more similar to what we would say in English such as *C'est un plaisir de faire votre connaissance*, which means it's a pleasure to meet you, as well as, *C'est un plaisir de vous connaître*, which means it's a pleasure to know you.

Whether you have just met someone or you meet up with someone who you know already, you can ask them how they are by saying *Comment allez-vous?* [coh-mon][ah-lay][v-oo-z], which means "how are you doing." This is a nice way of asking someone how they are doing. This would be used as a nicer and slightly more formal way of saying this, and if you want to ask your friend how they are by saying something more like "hey, how are ya?" or "what's up?" you would say *Ca va?* [sah][vah], this is used very commonly in French between friends as a replacement for "hi" and "how are you" at the same time. Similar to what we would say in English. If you want to ask someone specifically "what's new?" or "what's up?" you can ask this by saying *Quoi de neuf?* [k-wah][duh][n-uff], which directly translates to mean what is new? As a response to any of these, you can say the following;

Bien, et toi? Good, you? (less formal)
Bien, et vous? Good, you? (more formal)
Mal, et toi? Bad, you? (less formal)

Mal, et vous? Bad, you? (more formal)

Rien, toi? Nothing, you? (less formal)

Rien, vous? Nothing, you? (more formal)

As you begin the conversation with the person you have just met, you can say

Je suis [j-uh][s-wee], which means "I am." This would come in handy when you are getting to know someone, and you want to tell them more about yourself. This can be followed by just about anything that you want to say. For example, a feeling, an adjective or it can simply begin a sentence. An example is below.

Je suis heureux [j-uh][s-wee][euh-r-uh], which means "I am happy"

You can also begin a sentence by saying what you do for work or by asking the person what they do. *Je travaille comme dentiste,* which means "I work as a dentiste" or *je suis dentiste* "I am a dentist." You can ask them by saying *qu'est ce que vous faites comme travail* or *qu'est ce que tu fais comme travail?* The first example is a more formal way of asking, as it uses *vous* and the second is more casual. You will see more about occupations in another chapter later on in this book.

You will likely also need to know how to say yes, and no, as in a conversation, the other person will probably ask you at least a couple of yes or no questions.

Oui [wee], yes

Non [noh], no

If you are initiating a conversation with someone to whom you have not been introduced, you can get their attention by saying *Excusez-moi* [ex-k-you-z-ay][m-wah], which means "excuse me." This is a polite way to get someone's attention, and can also be used to ask someone to move aside politely if you need to get by them or if they are in your way. From this, a conversation may ensue which is when you would then introduce yourself and may ask them how they are doing, as you have learned above.

Please And Thank You

There are two different ways to say please in French. One of them is more formal than the other. As you learned previously in this book, there are two ways to tell *you,* as well. The word *vous* means "you" and is used in a much more formal way than *tu. Vous* can also be used in a plural sense to talk about people in terms of "you as a pair" or "you as a group" of people. If you have just met someone or if they are someone that you want to show respect to and be more formal with, then you will use the first example below. If you are friends with them and you want to say please in a more casual and less formal way, then you can use the second one.

S'il vous plait [seel][v-oo][play], please
S'il te plait [seel][t-uh][play], please

For example, you can put this together with the previous phrase to say "excuse me please" by saying *excusez-moi s'il vous plait*.

Thank You

When it comes to saying thank you in French, there are a few different ways to say this, depending on who you are talking to. There are more formal and less formal ways to say this, depending on who you are talking to.

Merci [meh-r-see], Thank you
Merci beaucoup [meh-r-see][b-oh-k-oo], Thanks a lot, thank you so much
Merci bien [meh-r-see][bee-yen], Thank you very much
If you want to be more formal, you can say thank you, sir, or thank you, ma'am.
Merci Madame [meh-r-see][mah-dah-m], Thank you ma'am

Merci Monsieur [meh-r-see][moh-see-uh-r], Thank you Sir

You can combine any of the above ways of saying thank you with sir or ma'am to be extra polite for example;

Merci Beaucoup Madame [meh-r-see][b-oh-k-oo][mah-dah-m], Thank you so much ma'am.

You're Welcome

To say you're welcome in French, we say "it's nothing" instead of saying you're welcome, but it means the same thing. Just like saying thank you, there is a variety of ways of saying you're welcome, depending on how formal or informal you prefer to be.

De rien, It's nothing.

Avec plaisir, with pleasure.

For the next two examples, you can see that there are two forms. The first is a less formal form because it uses the word *tu*. It looks different as it is made into a conjunction as t' instead of je *tu en* prie. The second example is more formal as it uses the word *vous* which is more formal

Je vous en prie

Je t'en prie

Chapter 9: Street Directions

Addresses

We will now look at the way we say addresses in French. When we are talking about street addresses, there many things that are different between French and English. First, we will break it up into pieces and look at each section contained in an address.

Streets

Rue [roo], Street
Route [roo-t], Road
Chemin [sh-uh-m-an], Trail, Path
Allee [ah-lay], Driveway
Ruelle [roo-el], Alley

Terrain de stationnement [tuh-r-an](rolled r)[duh][st-ah-si-on-mon-t], Parking lot

Numbers

You already know the numbers from one to beyond in French, and in this section, we will put that into practice. If you forget how to say the larger numbers that we learned in an earlier chapter, then for your purposes as long as you can say the numbers themselves you will be fine. I will show you an example of what I mean below.

325 Example St.

Instead of having to say Three hundred and twenty five example street, as long as you can say "three two five example street," you will be able to adequately get your point across to whoever you are asking like a taxi driver or a person from whom you are asking directions. As you now know, numbers from 1 to 20 and multiples of 10 from 20 to 100 (from learning about numbers in chapter 4), you will be able to say many many address numbers. If you aren't sure, however, you can simply state the numbers that you see that you do remember and the person you are talking to will likely be able to understand what you are trying to say. As a refresher, the numbers from 1 to 10 are again below for your reference.

1, 2, 3, 4, 5, 6, 7, 8, 9, 10

Un, deux, trois, quatre, cinq, six, sept, huit, neuf, dix

One, two, three, four, five, six, seven, eight, nine, ten

As an example, we will use the following address and look at it in more detail;

9 Rue Ste. Catherine

In French, when there is the word Saint, or St. in an address, like the street name *St. Catherine Street or St. Andrew street,* It is written as Ste. instead of St. like in English. This is because in French, the word is *Sainte.* So when talking about any word or street with the word Saint in it, it will be written in this way.

Ste. Catherine, Sainte Catherine
Ste. Andrew, Sainte Andrew

Address Examples

When we write addresses, we write them in this order; number + street type (road, crescent, etc.) + street name. It is a bit of a different order than in English as the word street is moved to the front of the street name instead of after it.

9 St. Catherine Street is what we would say in English. In French, this would be written as *9 Rue Ste. Catherine* and said as *neuf, rue sainte Catherine, à Paris, en France.*

13 Chemin Georges, un trois chemin georges, treize chemin georges. 13 Georges Street

100 chemin arbres, québec, québec, Canada. Cent chemin arbres, à québec, québec au Canada. 100 Arbres Trail, Quebec, Quebec, Canada.

À Kansas Vs. Au Kansas

When we are talking about being or having been someplace, there are different ways to say this, depending on what type of place it is you're talking about. For example, in the United States, there are two different places called Kansas. One is a state, and the other is a city. When speaking in English, we can tell which of these a person is talking about because if they are talking about the state they will say Kansas State. In French, we don't do this, but there is another way that we can actually tell which of these somebody is talking about based on the word that precedes it. If we are talking about a city or town, we would say **À Kansas,** which would indicate to the person we are speaking to that we are talking about the city. If we are talking about the state, we would say **Au Kansas.**

One more thing to note is that if the province, state or country we are talking about begins with a vowel, then using *au* would be quite a mouthful. In this case, we would say **en.** For example, "Je suis allé **en France**" which means I went to France. If you were talking about going to Paris, which is a city you would say "Je suis allé **à Paris**."

Asking For Directions

This section will focus on the phrases you will need when you are travelling. These are related to transportation and directions so that you can get around with ease.

If you need to ask someone where something is, you can ask them in the following way;

Excusez-moi, où est _____? This means Excuse me, where is _____? You will then insert something like *La Tour Eiffel*, The Eiffel Tower.

Like you learned earlier in this book, you could also say *Est ce que vous pouvez m'aider a trouver* _____? Which means, "could you help me find _____?"

Alternatively, you could also say *Est ce que vous savez ou est ce que c'est* _____? Which means, "Do you know where _____ is?"

After asking this, you will likely hear one of the following responses;

C'est à côté de [s-eh][ah][k-oh-tay][duh], It's beside (something)

C'est près de [s-eh][pr-eh][duh], It's close to (something)

C'est près d'ici [s-eh][pr-eh][d-ee-see]], It's close to here

C'est loin de [s-eh][l-w-ah-n][duh], It's far from (something)

C'est loin d'ici [s-eh][l-w-ah-n][d-ee-see], It's far from here

Left And Right

Gauche, Right
Droite, Left
C'est..., It is/ It's...
C'est à gauche, It's to the left

N,S,E,W

Below you will see the French terms for the compass directions North, South, East, and West. When using these in a sentence, you will say the word *vers*, which means *toward* or *in the direction of*. This is like saying "to the west" for example, in English.

North, *le nord,* [l-uh][n-or]
South, *le sud,* [l-uh][soo-d]
East, *l'est,* [l-ess-t]
West, *l'ouest,* [l-oo-ess-t]

Upstairs/Downstairs

When talking about directions in a house or a building, we will use the following terms.

En haut, Upstairs
En bas, Downstairs

We will now look at sentence examples of this.

Elle est allé en haut. She went upstairs.

Il aime aller en bas. He likes to go downstairs.

Chapter 10: Common Phrases For Travel

In this chapter, we are going to learn phrases that will be useful to you during travel and in order to get around with ease in new places, especially French-speaking places.

General Travel Phrases/ Asking For Travel Help

We will begin by learning some terms related to transportation so that you know how to put these words into a sentence.

Prendre..., To take...
Assurer la service, to ensure service

Venir, To come

Aller, To go

Arriver, To arrive

En Avance, Early

A l'heure, On time

En retard, Late

Buying A Ticket

This section will tell you how to buy a ticket and provide phrases that will help when you need to travel and find your way around transportation in general. We will look at a variety of scenarios, and you will be well on your way to traveling around with ease.

The first thing we will look at is the metro, the train or a bus. These types of transportation will require you to buy a ticket before you get on so you will need to know how to buy a ticket or how to ask for help if you aren't sure how. We will first look at some words that you will come across in the stations and on signs leading to these stations.

Un Billet [bee-yay], A Ticket

Les Billets, Tickets

You will likely see a sign that says, *Guichet de la Billetterie,* which means "Ticketing Counter." This is where you will go with your ticket questions or to buy a ticket. When you get to the counter, you will say *Bonjour, je voudrais acheter un billet,* which means, "Hello, I would like to buy a ticket." or *Un billet, s'il vous plaît.* "One ticket, please." If you want to get more specific, you can specify where exactly you are going so that you can be sure you will get a ticket to the right place. To do this, you will insert the name of the place you are going or the station you want to get to right after the word "ticket" like so; *Un billet <u>à Paris</u> s'il vous plaît.*

When it comes to buying tickets, if you are doing so at a counter or even online, the following terms will help you to ensure you clearly understand what you are buying so that you end up in the right place!

Un billet aller-retour, a return ticket

Un billet aller-simple, a one-way ticket

Je veux prendre le vol de huit heures. I would like to take the 8:00 flight.

Un siege, a seat

Je voudrais réserver un billet, I would like to reserve a ticket.

Je voudrais acheter deux billets pour New York. I would like to purchase two tickets to New York.

Payer par carte de crédit, pay via credit card

Combien coûte le billet? How much does the ticket cost?

Avez-vous un rabais pour les plus âgées? Do you have any discounts for seniors?

Avez-vous un rabais pour étudiants? Do you have any discounts for students?

A quelle heure est ce qu'on doit arriver? What time should we arrive?

When you are ready to go to the station for your train, bus or flight, you can say to your taxi driver one of the following;

Je dois aller au aeroport, I have to go to the airport
Est-ce que vous pouvais me conduire au station de train? can you drive me to the train station
Station de train, train station
Station d'autobus, bus station
Aeroport, Airport
Then, once you get to the station, you can ask for directions by saying;
Est-ce que vous pouvais m'aider a trouver mon gare? What this means is, "Can you help me find my gate?"
J'ai un vol pour attrapper, I have a flight to catch

Checking In

When checking into a flight, you would call this *enregistrer*.

If you want to ask someone where you can go to check into your flight, you can ask for *la reception*. If you want to tell someone that you are looking for the check-in desk, you can say *je veux me presenter a la reception*. Once you get there, you will want to tell them that you have a reservation. To say this, you will say *J'ai une reservation*.

Upon check-in, you will be able to ask any questions you may have, and you will be able to check your bags there. When they ask you which bags you want to check in you will say;

Nous avons cinq valises. We have five suitcases.

You can substitute this with any other number, as you learned previously in this book.

When you get to where you are going, you would say that you or someone else has;
Arriver, to arrive

More Travel Words And Phrases

Voyager, To travel

Un Passeport, A passport

Une Valise, A suitcase

Les bagages, baggage

Un plan, a map

Sortie, Exit

Entree, Entrance

Un Guide Touristique, A Tour Guide

Travel by Plane, Train Or Bus

Firstly, the car. This word you will likely use quite often in conversation as cars play such a big role in our lives both when travelling and when at home. There are actually two different ways that you can talk about a car. The first and more common is *Une Auto,* and the second is *Une Voiture.* Both of these mean "a car," but the second is regarded as the correct form. If you are speaking to people to whom you want to show respect or to those who you don't know quite as well, using the second option will be best. When speaking to friends, feel free to use *l'auto* when saying "the car." This word can be used for a vehicle in general but is reserved for more casual conversations.

Monospace, minivan
Convertible, convertible
Un camion, a truck

Avion, Airplane
Un hélicoptère, a helicopter
Le train, the train
L'autobus, the bus
Le Metro, The Subway/ The Metro
Un taxi, A taxi
Un ferry, A ferry

Une Navette, A shuttle

À pied, On foot
Un bateau, A boat
Un canot, A canoe
Une Planche à roulette, A Skateboard
Scooter, Scooter
Un bicyclette, A bicycle

If you are talking about taking one of these modes of transportation above, you would say *par* before it in a sentence, which means "by way of." For example, *par avion, par autobus,* or *par voiture.* These mean "by way of airplane," "by way of bus," and "by way of car," respectively.

Scenarios With Dialogue Examples

We will now learn how to use these in a sentence so that you can begin using these terms right away!

Ma petite amie est arrivée par planche À roulette hier, mais elle a été deux heures en retard! My girlfriend arrived by way of skateboard yesterday, but she was two hours late!

Un hélicoptère peut être un mode de transport très amusant! A helicopter could be a very fun mode of transport!

J'ai un bateau à moteur et un canot. Le bateau à moteur est beaucoup plus vite que le canot. I have a motor boat and a canoe. The motor boat is much faster than the canoe.

Le train est arrivé quinze minutes en avance et j'ai été heureux parce que j'ai voulu m'asseoir pendant que j'attendais le train quitter vers ma maison. The train arrived fifteen minutes early and I was happy because I wanted to sit down while I waited for it to leave for my house.

Chapter 11: Hotel And Accommodations

Firstly, we will learn some basic terms concerning hotels and accommodations.

Hôtel, hotel

Une Auberge, A Hostel

Lit, Bed

Chambre, room

Lit a une place, twin bed

Lit simple, twin bed

Lit deux places, double bed

Grand lit deux places, queen size bed

Un Lit King Size, A King size bed

Un Lit superposé, A Bunk Bed

La clé, the key

La clef, the key

Le premier étage, The First floor

Le deuxième étage, The Second floor

Le troisième étage, The Third floor

Le quatrième étage, The Fourth floor

L'ascenseur, the elevator

Booking A Hotel

When you go to a hotel, there are several things that you will want to know how to communicate so that you can ensure you get the experience you want. Being able to communicate about things like number of rooms, number of nights and the types of beds is very important.

To begin, when you find a hotel that you would like to stay in, you will likely begin by asking them if they have any vacancies. You can ask this by saying, *Avez-vous des chambres de disponible?* If they do, you can also ask them what rooms are available by saying *Quelles chambres avez-vous de disponible?*

Before this, though, when you are walking around looking for a place to stay, you may see a sign outside that says *Complet,* which means "no vacancy" or if they do have rooms available you may see either *Chambres de libres* or *De la place.* Both of these mean that the hotel has space available.

When you find a hotel, and they have rooms available, you can say the following phrases;

Est-ce que la chambre a de la climatisation? Does the room have air conditioning?

Je voudrais une chambre pour deux. I'd like a room for two

Je voudrais une chambre avec une douche. I'd like a room with a shower.

Est-ce que votre hôtel offre le service en chambre? Does your hotel offer room service?

Je voudrais une chambre non-fumeur s'il vous plaît. I would like a non-smoking room, please.

Est-ce que cet hôtel est loin de la gare? Is this hotel far from the train station?

Je voudrais rester dans une chambre avec un lit à une place. I'd like to stay in a room with a twin-size bed.

Je voudrais une chambre dans l'espace fumeur s'il vous plaît. I would like a room in the smoking section, please.

There may be some other interactions you would have with the front desk staff, like the following;

Once you have been assigned to a room and paid your cost, they will tell you, *Vous êtes dans la chambre numéro ____.* Meaning, "you are in room number ____."

They may tell you that *Vous devez régler la note avant midi.* Which is how we say, "You need to check out before noon" in French.

You may also need to cancel a booking you made. If this is the case, begin by saying, *Je voudrais annuler ma réservation, "I want to cancel my reservation."* they will then ask you for your name, and you should be all set! You can say this either over the phone or in person.

Chapter 12: Money

This chapter concerns money and how to talk about money. This will be useful in almost every interaction you have when travelling, like when booking things like hotels and tickets, when buying things in a store or when going to the bank.

Terms You Need To Know About Money

Money, l' Argent

La monnaie, Currency or change (depending on the context can be either)

Un billet, a bill (paper money)

Une piece, a coin

Un cheque, a cheque

Une carte, a card

More specifically,

Une carte bancaire, a bank card

Une carte de credit, a credit card

Payer, to pay

Payer en especes, pay in cash

Payer avec une carte bancaire, pay with a debit card

Acheter, to buy

Depenser, to spend

Un impot, tax

Going To The Bank

Une banque, A bank

Bancaire, banking

Un guichet automatique de banque, An ATM machine

Un compte, a bank account

épargne, Savings

Faire des économies, to save money

Un emprunt, a loan

Emprunter, to borrow

Signer, to sign

Le taux d'intérêt, an interest rate

Un dépôt, a deposit

Déposer, to deposit

Un virement, a transfer

Virer, to transfer

Un retrait, a withdrawal

Retirer, to withdraw

Toucher un chèque, to cash a cheque

Un relevé de compte, a bank statement

Les frais, fees

Un reçu, a receipt

Le bilan, a balance

Le montant, the amount

Currency exchange, un bureau de change

Le taux de change, Exchange rate

Changer de l'argent, to convert money

Une dette, a debt

Une action, A stock

Compter, to count

Gagner de l'argent, to earn money

Avoir besoin, to need

Le salaire, the wage

Le traitement, the salary

All of the words in the vocabulary list above can be used in a sentence when speaking about money or currency. You can use these terms along with the verbs you learned earlier in this book in order to make any sentence you like about money.

Chapter 13: The Hospital

Emergency Help Phrases

In a medical emergency, it can be hard to remember a language that is not your first. Remember the following few phrases just in case you are ever in this situation.

Au secours! Help!

Aidez-moi, Help me

Urgence, The Emergency Room

J'ai eu un accident, I had an accident

L'Hopital, The hospital

J'ai besoin d'un médecin, I need a doctor

Ou est-ce que je peux trouver une clinique médicale? Where can I find a medical clinic?

Une trousse de premiers secours, A First-Aid Kit

Below are some phrases that you may hear the doctor or someone else who is helping you asking you in an emergency. They may also tell you some of these things as a statement.

Qui dois-je contacter? Who should I contact?

Vous avez... You have...

Mon diagnostique est... My diagnosis is...

Prenez votre médicament ____ fois par jour pendant _____ jours. Take your medication _____ times a day for _____ days.

Medical Terms

When visiting the doctor, the following terms and phrases will help you to ensure you understand the doctor and that the doctor understands you as well. The following terms are things that you may need to tell the doctor about how you are feeling, or things that they may ask you about how you are feeling. First, however, the doctor will likely ask you some questions in the form of a sentence when they first see you. Some common examples of this are below.

Qu'est-ce qui ne va pas? What's wrong?

Que sont vos symptomes? What are your symptoms?

Ou est-ce que c'est le douleur? Where is the pain?
Est-ce que ca fait mal? Does this hurt?

Est-ce que je peux vous toucher ici? Can I touch you here?

Question: *Est-ce que c'est la première fois que ceci vous est arrivé? Is this the first time this has happened to you?*
Answer: *Oui, yes* or *Non, no.*

Est-ce que vous avez des allergies? Do you have any allergies?

After hearing one or more of these questions, you can answer with any number of the following;

J'ai mal, I'm in pain
Je ne vais pas bien, I'm not feeling well
Bras/ jambe/ poignet brisee, Broken arm/leg/wrist
Il y a du saignement, There is bleeding
J'ai une blessure, I have an injury
J'ai une Fièvre, I have a fever
Il y a du gonflement, There is swelling
Je pense que j'ai une Maladie, I think I have a sickness/ an illness

Hospital Terms

Sang, blood

Assurance medicale, medical insurance

Un bleu, a bruise

Diagnostic, Diagnosis

Une Infirmiere, a female nurse

Un infirmier, a male nurse

Une pharmacie, a pharmacy

Une Radiographie, An X-ray

Une Pilule, A pill

How To Make An Emergency Call

If you are in europe, or France more specifically, there are different numbers you would call to reach emergency services. In North America, you would call 911, while in Europe you would call 112. This will connect you to the general emergency number of Europe. If you know that there has been an accident or something that needs immediate fire services such as people needing a rescue or something like a gas leak, you can call 18 instead. If someone is in grave danger, such as a heart attack or a serious injury, you will call 15 to directly be connected to emergency medical services that will send someone immediately to help you. But once you call, you will need to know what to say. This section will teach you exactly what to say so that you can make an emergency call while abroad if you need to, which hopefully will never happen.

When calling 18 to reach fire services, you may need to say something like this;

Il y a eu un accident de voiture. There has been a car accident.
Elle est gravement blessée. She is seriously injured.
Il y a eu une explosion de gaz. There has been a gas explosion.

When calling 15 to reach emergency medical services, you may need to say something like this;

Elle ne respire plus. she has stopped breathing.
J'ai besoin d'une ambulance, I need an ambulance
Il est inconscient, He is unconscious

If there is someone near you and you cannot call, you can ask them to call 15 by saying
"S'il vous plait, appelez une ambulance. Please call for an ambulance."

If you are talking on the phone to the emergency medical dispatcher, they may ask you some things like

Ou est ce que vous êtes? Where are you?

Est-il conscient? Is he conscious?

C'est quoi son nom? What is his name?

Je vais envoyer l'ambulance, I will send the ambulance.

An emergency call may go something like this;

Chapter 14: Shopping

Shopping Terms

Faire du shopping, To shop/ To go shopping

Faire du lèche-vitrine, to window shop/ To go window shopping

Une Solde, A Sale

Portefeuille, Wallet

Bon Shopping! Happy shopping/ enjoy shopping!

Acheter, to buy

Vendre, to sell

Store Types

Un Grand Magasin, A department store

Un Centre commerciale, A shopping mall

181

Un marché, a market

How to ask for assistance

Est-ce que c'est en solde? Is this on sale?

Bon marché, Good deal/ cheap

Meilleur marché que..., A better deal than...

Une bonne affaire, A good deal

C'est combien? How much does this cost?

Ou sont les cabines? Where are the change rooms?

Est-ce qu'il y a un miroir? Is there a mirror?

Je vais essayer... I am going to try on...

C'est trop serre, it's too tight

J'aime celui-ci le plus. I like this one the best

I like this a lot. Ce me plait beaucoup

I am going to get this, je vais le prendre

I want to buy this one. J'ai envie d'acheter celui-ci

Vous fermez à quelle heure? What time do you close?

Vous êtes ouvert demain? Are you open tomorrow?

If you are looking for something specific, you can also ask the employee to help you find this. For example, if you are looking at a shirt that you like but you want to know if they have any other sizes or colors, you can ask them this by saying *Est-ce que vous l'avez...* This means "do you have it..." You will insert whatever you like in place of the three dots. Some examples of this are below.

Est-ce que vous l'avez en rouge?

Est-ce que vous l'avez en taille petit?

Est-ce que vous l'avez en taille 29?

Notice how the word *taille* is used here; this means "size." If you are looking for a certain size, you will say "size small"

I am going to pay. Je vais à la caisse

Est-ce que je peux avoir un sac en plastique? Can I have a plastic bag?

Est-ce que je peux avoir un sac en papier? Can I have a paper bag?

Est-ce que vous prenez les cartes de crédit? Do you take credit cards?

Est-ce que je peux payer par carte bancaire? Can I pay by debit card?

Je voudrais échanger celui-ci s'il vous plaît, I want to exchange this please

Je voudrais retourner celui-ci, I want to return this one

What The Cashier/Staff May Ask You

A store employee may come up and ask you if you need any help by saying *Est-ce que je peux vous aider?* Which means, can I help you? They may also ask you something like *Vous cherchez quelque chose?* Which means "Are you looking for something?" You can respond in a number of ways, one of which is by saying *Non, merci, je regarde simplement.* What this means is "No thank you, I'm just looking" or I'm just browsing." If you do want help, you can say *Oui, merci. Je cherche...*This means "yes, thank you, I am looking for..." Then you will insert whatever you are looking for. Examples of this are below.

Oui merci, je cherche une robe noir. Yes, thank you. I am looking for a black dress.

Oui merci, je cherche des/les souliers. Yes, thank you, I am looking for (the) shoes

Oui merci, je cherche les lunettes de soleil. Yes, thank you, I am looking for the sunglasses.

Oui merci, je cherche un cadeau pour ma petite amie. Yes, thank you. I am looking for a gift for my girlfriend.

Chapter 15: Common Phrases For Conversation In Real Life Situations

Who What When Where Why And How

Qui?, Who?

Où? Where?

Comment? How?

Quand? When?

Qu'est-ce que? What?

Pourquoi? Why?

These words can be used to start a conversation with a stranger, to ask someone a question, or to get more information for yourself from just about anyone.

Conversation Starters

Combien? How much?

Quel ___ préférez-vous? Which ___ do you prefer?

Quel, Which? (masculine form)

Quelle? Which? (feminine form)

Comment s'appelle le garcon? What is the boy's name?

Comment s'appelle ___? What's ___ name?

Qui est-ce? Who is it?

Qu'est-ce que tu fais? What are you doing? (informal)

Où habitez-vous? Where do you live?

Pourquoi allez-vous à ___? Why are you going to ___?

Quel est son prénom? What's his/her first name?

Ce n'est pas grave! That's okay

Chapter 16: Common Phrases For Everyday Use

In this chapter, we will look at even more common phrases that you can use in everyday conversations. We will begin with texting in French.

Texting In French

In French, when you are texting, it is called "un texto" [t-ex-toh]. There are some short-forms you can use when texting in French, and French-speaking people will know what you mean. If you are texting a French-speaking person, you may see some of these short forms if they are sending you text messages.

Bsr, bonsoir, *good evening, good night*

biz, bisous, *kisses*

sa va, sa va? Or sa va.

If it's used as a question, it means *are you good?* Or *how are you?*

If it is used as a statement, it means *I'm good,* or *it's going well.*

b1, bien , *good*

é twa, et toi, *and you?, how are you?*

dsl, je suis désolé, *I'm sorry*

Both of the next two short forms mean see you later or see you soon, but one is a little more polite than the other. The second form would be used more casually when texting friends.

a tt, à toute à l'heure, *see you soon, see you later*

a +, à plus, *see you later*

The next two examples are two ways of saying, please, just like we learned earlier. One of them, the one that uses *vous* is a more formal way. Sometimes you may be texting someone with whom you want to be a bit more respectful, and this is when you would use this one. The one that uses *tu* is a less formal form and one that you would use with a friend.

stp, s'il te plaît, *please (informally)*

svp, s'il vous plaît, *please (formally)*

Phrases You Will Use The Most

Bonjour [bon-j-oor], Hello, hi

Without a doubt, the most common words you will use will be bonjour (hello) and thank you (merci). You have already learned some of these words, but in this section, we will put all of the words you know now together in one place for you to reference later! The focus of this section will be the different forms of common phrases. You will need to pay attention to whom you are speaking to and decide if you should be more formal or less formal, depending on your relationship. When in doubt, choose the more formal option, and they may tell you that you can be less formal with them.

Informal Vs. Formal Forms Of Common Phrases

As you may remember, there are actually two quite different ways to say please in the French language. One of them is more formal than the other. As you learned previously in this book, there are two ways to tell *you,* as well. The word *vous* means you and is used in a much more formal way than *tu. Vous* can also be used in a plural sense to talk about people in terms of you as a pair or a group of people. If you have just met someone or if they are someone that you want to show respect to and be more formal with, then you will use the first example below. If you are friends with them and you want to say please in a more casual and less formal way, then you can use the second one.

S'il vous plait [seel][v-oo][play], please
S'il te plait [seel][t-uh][play], please

Je suis [j-uh][s-wee], I am.
This can be followed by just about anything that you learned in the previous chapters. You can follow it with a feeling, an adjective or it can simply be the beginning of a sentence.

Tu es [too][ay], you are.
This is similar to the previous example that means I am, but when you are speaking to someone in a less formal and more casual way, you would say you are... For a more formal and respectful way of saying you are, you can use the word vous instead of tu and adjust the verb etre accordingly, making it Vous etes [voo-s][eh-tt-s].

Je m'appelle [j-uh][m-ah-p-el], My name is. This directly translates to mean, "I am called."

Enchanté [on-sh-on-tay], Nice to meet you. You would say this right after meeting someone new, just like how we would say "it's nice to meet you" or "pleasure to meet you" in English.

Pardon? [pa-r-doh-n] (rolled r), Pardon?, Sorry? Sorry. This can be used in a variety of ways, either to ask someone politely to repeat themselves or as a statement if you wish to apologize to someone. You can use this when you are squeezing by someone at the movie theatre when you go to the bathroom during the film if you want someone to repeat what they said because you didn't hear them or if you want to apologize to someone.

Comment t'appelles-tu? [coh-mon][t-app-el][t-oo], What is your name? This is similar to the above examples where vous can be switched out if you are speaking to a group of people or if you want to be more formal. In this case, you would say comment vous appelez-vous? [coh-mon][v-oo-z][app-el-ay][v-oo-z], though the English translation of these is the exact same.

Oui [wee], yes

Non [noh], no

Comment allez-vous? , How are you? This is a nice way of asking someone how they are doing, as it uses the word *vous*.

Ca va? is something that we use when we want to ask someone, "how are you," but this is more like saying, "hey, how are ya?" or "what's up?" This would be used with friends.

Excusez-moi, excuse me. This can be used to get someone's attention in a polite way, and can also be used to ask someone to move if you need to get by them or if they are in your way. This is a way of saying either of these things politely.

Je ne comprends pas; I don't understand. I hope you won't need to use this one too much, but if you don't understand someone's French when they are speaking too fast, or if you don't understand a concept in general aside from the language you can say this to them.

If you need to ask someone how to say a certain thing in French, you can ask them, Comment dit-on ... en francais? And then insert the thing that you are asking them about. For example, you can ask them, "comment dit-on banana en francais? how do you say banana in French?

In French, if we want to say see you later, we would say *à toute à l'heure* [ah][too-t][ah][l-err]. If you want to say see you later, on a specific day, we would say, for example, "see you Tuesday," à mardi!

If you want to ask someone for help for anything you can say
"Est-ce que vous pouvez m'aider?" which means "Can you help me?"

If a question is asked that you do not know, you can say "Je ne sais pas" [j-uh][nuh][say][pah] which means "I don't know."

If you were to ask someone about something, what something is, or if you need clarification about something specific you can say "Qu'est-ce que c'est?" which means What is it? Or It can also mean what is _____. You then will insert whatever you are wondering about such as

Qu'est-ce que c'est ca? "Which means what is that?"

You can substitute this for anything by doing the following;

Qu'est-ce que c'est (insert word in French that you aren't sure of the meaning of), this could be something like Qu'est-ce que c'est *l'hiver?* If you're unsure of the word that they just said. Then, they will tell you that *l'hiver* means *winter.*

Chapter 17: Short Stories For Beginners

This chapter contains short stories in French for you to practice everything you have learned in real sentences and scenarios. These stories are meant to be a fun way for you to put all of the knowledge you have gained in this book together in once place and hopefully read these stories through with as much understanding of the basic concepts as possible. As you practice your French language skills more and more, your story comprehension will improve as well. Then, you can come back to these stories and hopefully discover something new about them!

Story Number 1

For the first story, it will be written out for you in English first so that you can get an idea of what to expect from the story. Then, read through it in French to practice your French reading skills. This first story is called The Lumberjack or Le Bûcheron in French.

The Lumberjack

There is a lumberjack who lives in the woods and is cutting a tree near the river one day. While chopping down the tree, he drops his axe into the river.

The river is so deep that he can't see to the bottom, and he cannot see his axe at all. He doesn't know how he will get his axe back, so he sits on the edge of the river and begins to cry.

All of a sudden, a god appears. He says that he is called the god of rivers. The god of rivers asks the lumberjack why he is crying, and the lumberjack tells him that he has lost his axe at the bottom of the river.

The god then dives into the river to get the axe. After a few minutes, the lumberjack starts to get worried because the god is still down there, and the river is so deep. Then, the god surfaces. He has come back with an axe made of gold.

"Thank you, but that's not mine." Says the lumberjack

The god puts the axe down and dives into the river again. After a few minutes, he surfaces, and when he comes up he has an axe made of silver in his hand.

"I'm sorry, but that's not mine either." Says the lumberjack

The god dives in again, and this time, he comes up to the surface and out of the water with an axe made of iron in his hand.

"My axe!" The lumberjack exclaims excitedly.

It turns out that the god of rivers is very impressed with the lumberjack's honesty. He is happy and proud that the lumberjack did not lie in order to take either of the axes that were of much more value than his own- gold and silver being much more valuable than iron. As a reward, the god of rivers gives the lumberjack the axe made of gold and the axe made of silver as well as his own axe. The lumberjack accepts the reward graciously.

The moral of this story is that when we are honest, despite being in a position where we could easily lie and earn something we may really like to have, the universe rewards us in big ways. Honesty is always the best choice, and it comes back to help you later on in even better ways than if you had lied in the first place. You gain a bigger reward from being honest than from taking what you want with dishonesty. When we are honest, people can see that we are genuine, and they want to be our friends as a result.

Le Bûcheron

Un bûcheron qui vit au foret coupe les arbres chaque jour avec le même axe. Cet axe est son possession le plus précieux car il l'utilise chaque jour pour faire son travaille.

Un jour, son axe tombe dans le rivière quand il est en train de couper un arbre très proche du rivière. Le rivière est très très profond, et il ne peut pas voir son axe du tout! Il ne peut pas voir le fond du rivière, alors il ne sait pas comment le sauver et c'est pour ca qu'il ne peut pas récupérer son axe. Il devient triste et il s'assit au bord du rivière et il commence a pleurer.

Tout à coup, un dieu apparaît. Le dieu dit qu'il est appelé le dieu des rivières. Le dieu demande au bûcheron,

«pourquoi est-ce que vous pleurez?

- J'ai perdu mon axe! Dit le bûcheron. c'est tombé dans la rivière et je ne peux pas le voir.

-attends mon gars.»

Le dieu des rivières saute dans l'eau et il va assez profond que le bûcheron ne peut pas lui voir sous l'eau. Il devient peur. Une minute plus tard, le dieu fait surface. Dans son main, il a une axe fait complètement de l'or.

«Je vous remercie, mais ça ce n'est pas mon axe.»

Le dieu plonge encore dans l'eau, et quand il fait surface ce fois, il a dans son main une axe fait complètement de l'argent.

«Je suis désolé, mais ça ce n'est pas mon axe non plus.»

Encore une fois, le dieu plonge au fond du rivière pour récupérer l'axe du bûcheron. Quelques minutes plus tard, le dieu fait surface et dans son main il tient une axe fait de fer. Ce fois, le bûcheron dit,

«C'est mon axe! Vous avez trouvé mon axe!»

Le dieu est très fier du bûcheron car il n'a pas accepter les axes avec beaucoup plus de valeur que l'axe fait de fer qui appartient vraiment au bûcheron. Pour son honnêteté, le dieu veut lui donner une récompense. Le dieu donne le bûcheron l'axe fait d'or et l'axe fait d'argent comme cadeau.

Le leçon dans cet histoire c'est que quand on est honnête, nous sommes récompensés par l'univers dans des façons gros. Quand on est honnête à propos de quelque chose, même si on peut recevoir quelque chose qu'on veut, on peut recevoir des récompenses très grand pour choisir le bon choix. Quand nous décidons de ne pas mentir, les gens peuvent voir que nous sommes genuine et gentille et ils veulent être nos amies comme résultat.

Story Number 2

For this second story, it is written in French first, followed by its English translation. This time, read through the story in French first and try to understand as much as you can. Then, once you have done this, read through the English version and see how close your comprehension was when reading it in French first.

L'Arbre

Il y a des vingtaines d'ans, un garçon qui a été très pauvre. Sa famille n'a pas eu assez d'argent pour acheter les jouets ou les choses pour lui de s'amuser avec. Pendant le majorite de son vie, il a dû lui amuser toute seul. Il avait une soeur, mais elle aimait jouer au rivière et le garçon n'aimait pas devenir mouillé alors il ne voulait pas le joindre jamais. C'est pour ca qu'il passait la plupart de son temps au parc qui a été proche de son appartment. Il a joué des jeux imaginaires dans le gazon, ou il a grimper les arbres pour voir toute ce qui se passait en dessous de lui.

Un jour au milieu de l'été, quand il marchait dans le parc comme d'habitude, il a vu un arbre très grand qu'il n'a pas reconnaît comme un arbre qu'il a déjà vu. Il savait qu'il aurait rappelé cette arbre car il a essayé à grimper toutes les arbres très grandes et s'il a vu cette arbre déjà, il aurait essayé de le grimper. Il savait aussi parce que sur le devant de l'arbre, il y avait une signe de papier sur qui était écrit *Je suis un arbre magique. Si vous disiez le charme, vous allez voir le magique.*

Le garçon est devenu très excité, parce qu'il s'est passé chaque jour au parc et il n'a jamais vu un arbre comme ca. Cette arbre a été beaucoup plus grand que tous les autres arbres en ville et il n'a jamais vu une arbre magique. Il aimait beaucoup les arbres et une arbre magique était une rêve pour lui.

Il pensait de tous les trucs magiques qu'il a déjà entendu parler. Car il n'a pas eu une télévision pour regarder les programmes avec des sorcières, il n'a pas su beaucoups de sorts magiques. Il a essayé a rappelé qu'est ce que ses amies ont dises quand ils ont joués les jeux avec les sorcières ou les magiciens. Qu'est qu'ils disent quand ils jettent les sorts? Pense le garcon.

Le garçon a essayé tous les charmes qu'il a pu pensé. Il a dit *abracadabra, sésame, ouvre-toi* et tous les autres qu'il est entendu dans son vie, mais rien n'a pas marché. Il a essayé pendant toute la journée! Il est devenu très fatigué. Il s'assoit sur le gazon sous l'arbre et il a cri,

«S'il te plait! Cheri arbre!»

Tout à coup, une porte géant est ouvert dans le tronc de l'arbre. Le garçon a été très confus, mais il a été contente que l'arbre est ouvert finalement. Le garçon est entré dans le tronc de l'arbre et tout était noir dedans. La porte d'où il est devenu pour entrer dans le tronc de l'arbre a fermé maintenant et le garçon est devenu un peu peur dans le noir. Il cherche pour une façon de quitter, mais il ne pouvait pas voir rien.

Il n'a pas pu voir rien mais en cherchant, il a vu finalement un signe sur le papier blanche qui disait *continuer avec ton magique.*

Le garçon a lu le signe et il lui a demandé à quoi faire maintenant. Il a essayé encore ses mots magiques comme *abracadabra,* et *sésame, ouvre-toi* et toutes les autres qu'il pouvait rappeler dans ce moment de peur. Car il ne savait pas laquelle a réussi à ouvrir la porte la dernière fois, Il ne savait pas exactement quoi dire et maintenant il ne savait pas quoi d'autre il pouvait faire. Il s'assit sur le plancher et il pense. Il ne sait pas quoi faire, mais le seul chose qu'il sait c'est qu'il a senti très contente que l'arbre a ouvert sa porte le première fois alors il a dit,

«Merci! Cheri arbre! Merci pour ouvrir ton porte pour moi la première fois»

Tout à coup, l'intérieur du tronc à illuminée et le garçon a pu voir encore! Il a souri. Il regardait partout pour voir ou il était et il a vu un chemin rouge qui brillait devant lui. Le garçon a été surpris et très excité qu'il a réussi encore.

Le garçon a suivi le chemin et a la fin du chemin était un tas énorme formée de toutes sorts de chocolats et de jouets!

Car le garçon n'a jamais eu ses propres jouets dans toute son vie et il n'a pas eu assez d'argent pour les chocolats, il a été très excitée par ce récompense.

Au bout de la Tronc, en haut de tous les chocolates et les jouets était un signe dernier qui disait *s'il vous plaît et merci sont les mots magiques.*

Le garçon a été très heureux d'avoir trouvé les mots magiques.

Les jours qui ont suivi, Il a apporté tous ses amis et sa soeur à l'arbre et il les a instruire comment ouvrir l'arbre par dire les mots *s'il vous plaît* et *merci.* Il a voulu que toutes les enfants pouvaient jouer avec des jouets et manger du chocolate alors il a partager tous avec eux. Ils ont eu une gros fête plein de chocolats et de jouets dans l'arbre.

Rappelles-toi, les mots magiques sont toujours *s'il vous plaît* et *merci.*

Fin

Le leçon dans cette histoire, c'est que les mots magiques dans n'importe quel situation sont s'il vous plaît et merci. Comme en anglais, il y a des mots magiques en francais aussi.

L'autre leçon c'est que partager avec les amis est toujours plus amusant que garder tout pour toi. Même si le garçon n'avait pas beaucoup de choses, il a voulu partager avec ses amis et sa soeur pour qu'ils pouvaient les amuser aussi.

Le dernier leçon c'est la persévérance. Le garçon est devenu peur quand il n'y avait pas de lumière et il a ete tres fatiguee apres essayer toutes les mots magiques qu'il savait, mais il a persévéré pendant longtemps et les récompenses ont vaut le coût définitivement!

The Tree

Many many years ago, there was a boy who was very poor. His family didn't have enough money for toys or candy or anything like that. He didn't have much to do at home, so he spent most of his days in the park near his house.

One day while he was walking in the park, he saw a huge tree with a sign on the front of it that read: *say the magic words and you will see the magic.*

As he spent most of his time in the park, he would have noticed this tree before if it had been here, he thought. He decided to try to find out what the magic words were.

The boy tried all of the magic words he could think of like *abracadabra* and *Open Sesame* and all others he could think of. He had been trying all day, and nothing worked yet. By this point, he had become very tired.

He sat on the ground at the base of the tree and yelled, exasperated, "Please! Dear tree!"

Suddenly a giant door opened in the trunk of the tree. The boy entered the tree trunk, and it was completely dark inside except for another sign that read: *Continue with your magic.* The boy wasn't sure which magic word had worked in the end, so he tried them all again. Nothing worked, but he was feeling quite thankful that the tree had opened its trunk in the first place, so he said "Thank you! Dear tree."

All of a sudden, the inside of the trunk illuminated, and a red pathway was shining before him. The boy was very excited!

The boy followed the pathway, and at the end of it was a huge pile of chocolate and toys. At the very end of the trunk, there was one final sign that read. *Please, and Thank you are the magic words.*

The boy was so excited that he had figured out the magic words. He had never had toys or chocolate, so he was over the moon! He went back to the tree the next day, but this time he brought his friends and his sister with him. He taught them tall what the magic words were, and showed them that saying them in the right order opened the tree trunk. He and his friends had a big party in the tree trunk, and everyone had so much fun.

Remember, the magic words are always *please* and *thank you*!

The moral of this story is that The magic words in any situation are always please and thank you. These can be said anytime, anywhere, and you will get positive reactions. These reactions may not be toys and chocolate, but they will be people's happiness and kindness.

The second moral of this story is that everything is better when shared with friends and family. The boy didn't have much, but he still wanted to share the gifts he received with his friends and his sister. He wanted to share the reward because he wanted everyone else to be able to enjoy it, too, and he thought it would be more fun to share this reward with them. Generosity with friends makes the experience that much better.

Conclusion

Thank you for reaching the end of the book *French Made Easy*. Hopefully, this book was able to demonstrate for you how easy it can be to learn the French language when it is laid out for you in the right way. This book finished with a few short stories so that you could practice everything you have learned by trying to read through a piece of text that contained everything you learned all in one place. From here, you can now go on to find more short stories to read in order to practice your French language skills.

Like I mentioned in the introduction to this book, when it comes to learning a language, practice is key. This means to practice in the form of exposure, as well. Your brain is able to pick up on things even if they are not in your conscious mind, so even having a French audiobook on in the background while you clean the house or do grocery shopping will help you to remember everything you have learned, especially the pronunciations.

The next best thing to do will be to find people to practice with. Whether these people are your friends who are also interested in learning the French language, or you find a pen pal across the world, being able to practice your French with other people is a great way to brush up on your skills and get feedback from other people in real-time. This avoids bad habits and confusion, as there is someone else to bounce your French off of. If you do not have access to this, reading books and watching movies is a great place to start. Beginning with children's books of short stories will help you to start out slow, and as your vocabulary grows, you can progress to harder books in terms of grammar and word choice.

Do not get discouraged if some days become difficult or some days, it is harder to remember the language. Patience will be necessary for you as you are learning, as with anything else. You do not become an expert overnight but the earlier you start practicing, the earlier you will get there. Try to find people to keep you motivated and try to enjoy the learning as it comes. One day you will blurt out an entire French sentence when travelling in France and you will surprise yourself. You will also be glad that you read this book and that you practiced your French language skills so often.

If you would like, share this book with your friends and family and plan a trip to France together! This will not only serve as motivation to study and practice, but it will give you all other people to practice with in the meantime.

Exposing yourself to as many new forms of language as possible is hugely beneficial, as your brain is eager to learn and grow. Language is a beautiful thing in this world, and we should take advantage of the many resources available to us that allow us to enrich our lives with it.

Spanish

Made

Easy

Common Phrases for Beginners for Travel and Conversation. Learn to Speak and Understand Fluent Spanish Dialogues. Practical Step-By-Step Grammar, Reading and Writing Exercises.

By Carol Carlson

Table of Contents

Introduction

Learning a foreign language is a goal that many people all around the world have tried to achieve. From children to adults, more and more people want the longed-for fluency in a language that most can use on a day-to-day basis. Not only that, in a more globalized and interconnected world, it's crucial to know a second language if someone wants to improve academically and have more opportunities in the job market.

But what if you're just learning a foreign language as a hobby, for fun, or to communicate with friends, relatives or neighbors? Well, you still need to get through all the learning and lessons needed. No matter the reason you're learning a foreign language, you will have to put forth earnest effort and practice as much as you can.

A language that has proven to be useful is Spanish. The Spanish language, as we know it today, has evolved and changed a lot since it first became popular in the Iberian Peninsula in the westernmost part of Europe in the 1500s. To lovers of ancient and medieval history, the Spanish language is a treasure ready to be discovered. Nowadays, Spanish is the official language in more than 25 countries and is used by more than 420 million native speakers found in Europe, Latin America and even Asia. This, in turn, makes Spanish one of the most-spoken languages in the world. You might also find it interesting to know that Spanish is one of the six official languages used in the UN.

With all of this in mind, it's easy to understand why many people are attracted to learn how to speak this beautiful language. Its usefulness stands out among many other languages. You might even know some people who have Spanish as a native tongue and long to communicate with them. You might want to travel to a Spanish-speaking country within a couple of weeks and need a guide to the most common and useful, modern phrases.

If so, then *Spanish Made Easy* is the book you have been looking for. *Spanish Made Easy* is more than just a language book. It's a tool that will help you develop your language skills in a way you've never tried before. This book consists of 4 chapters. Each one of them is further divided into more small and easy-to-digest sections. Each section deals with important topics and provides the necessary vocabulary so that you can easily enjoy learning Spanish.

At the end of each chapter, you'll find exercises that will help solidify the previously-acquired knowledge. These exercises are important, and you'll benefit a lot if you strive to solve them. Results are provided at the end of the book and you can check them any time you want.

Whatever you reason to learn Spanish, you're encouraged to continue learning and not give up. Don't come to think that the path to fluency is a rocky one. Granted, it might take longer than you expected, but with enough effort and perseverance, you can learn the beautiful language that is Spanish, and come to enjoy it!

Chapter 1: Tips and Tricks to Speak and Understand Spanish

Spanish has a lot of history. This is not just a simple statement. Due to its long history, it has changed. As a direct "descendant" of the Latin language, Spanish shares a lot of vocabulary and even grammatical structures with other Romance languages like Portuguese, French, Italian, Catalan, and Romanian. The Iberian Peninsula, where Spanish had its beginnings, was once occupied by Arabic speakers, and so many words used today by Spanish speakers have Arabic roots.

To drive the point home, Spanish, like any other language, can be somewhat tricky to understand at first, but, like any other language, there are tips you can use to understand it. Accent is one important factor you need to have in mind.

What's an accent? Simply put, an accent is a way a person speaks any language. Most of the time, you may have seen this being portrayed on TV or in films where foreigners try to speak English and, even though they do so somewhat clearly, they have a very distinct way to pronounce certain words and maybe even different ways to construct sentences.

Throughout the Spanish-speaking world, you'll find a lot of accents. A person from Spain doesn't have the same accent as a person from South America. Spanish speakers usually say that Latin Americans have a very particular *seseo,* that is, the tendency to pronounce the letters *c* and *z* as the letter *s,* which means they don't stress the difference when these letters are used in a word. On the other hand, Latin Americans might readily recognize a European Spanish if he starts emphasizing those letters and by his intonation when asking.

Some words and phrases, at least colloquially, are used differently in Spanish countries. In other words, a person from Spain uses some particular words when speaking; another person from South America might refer to the same thing using another word; and so on. One clear example of this is the word *muchacho,* which can be translated into English as *guy:* in Spain, you might hear a guy is being called *chaval,* in Venezuela, *chamo*; in Peru, *chibolo;* and so on.

These differences shouldn't scare you. These differences actually enrich the language and make it stand out. While there are many differences in accents and in the usage of certain words, most Spanish speakers, no matter where they come from, can understand each other without any problems.

One good tip to learning Spanish is being exposed to it as much as possible. Do you have to be close to a Spanish speaker all the time? Of course not, but don't overestimate the chance to practice with a native speaker. Being close to native speakers will let you hear and see how they use the language in a conversation. Do you need to choose a particular variety of Spanish when deciding which one to learn? Not necessarily, but it's up to you. Some people prefer the variety that comes from Argentina; others prefer the one from Spain; still, others prefer to pick vocabulary from each variety and set out to learn as much as they can from all the varieties. Just have this in mind, no matter what variety you choose, you'll be completely understood. *Spanish Made Easy* provides a standard vocabulary, but it's one that all Spanish speakers can understand.

Exposition to the language can be achieved by watching TV news in Spanish, listening to the radio, reading some magazines or newspapers in Spanish, or volunteering in an international or Spanish organization. That's the end and purpose of a language that you come to use it with the people who have it as a native tongue. So, don't give up on exposing yourself to the language and you'll notice how fast you can learn.

One of the things that you can first learn to understand this language, though, is the alphabet. Let's see the Spanish alphabet and its pronunciation.

The Spanish Alphabet

The Spanish Alphabet is not really different from the one English speakers use. It has 27 letters. These are:

- A, pronounced as the letter *a* in the English word *cat*
- B, pronounced as the letter *b* in the English word *bat*
- C has 2 pronunciations in Spanish. Before the vowels, *a,o,* and *u,* the letter *c* is pronounced as it sounds in *cat, come* and *cool.* But, before the vowels *e* and *i,* the pronunciation of the letter *c* is as in *certain* and *cylinder.*
- D, pronounced as it appears in *day*
- E, pronounced as it appears in *elephant.*
- F, pronounced as it appears in *fail.*
- G has 2 pronunciations. Before the vowels *e* and *i,* it's pronounced as the letter *h* in words like *heroe* and *hills.* Before the vowels *a, o* and *u,* it's pronounced as in the words *gallon, goal* and *gummy.* In addition, the letter *u* is added between the letters *g* and *e/i* to have that latter pronunciation, forming *gue* and *gui.* These can be pronounced just like the letter *g* when it's used in English words like *guess* and *guilty.*
- H is mostly considered a "mute" letter. This means that most of the time, this letter doesn't have any sound. Of course, there are exceptions to these. The letter *h* can

be placed after the letter *c* to form *ch*. *Ch* is pronounced as is appears in *Charlie, chocolate,* and *chamber*.

- I, pronounced as *ee* when it appears in words like *feet* or *greet*.

- J, pronounced as *h* when it appears in words like *home* or *hello*.

- K, pronounced as it appears in *kilo, koala,* and *kiss*.

- L, pronounced as it appears in *Lola, lab,* and *lorry*. The letter *l* can also be duplicated, forming *ll*. The double letter *ll* is pronounced as the letter *y* when it appears in words like *yes* and *yawn*.

- M, pronounced as it appears in *mom*.

- N, pronounced as it appears in *nanny* or *nothing*.

- Ñ, which is a special letter only used in Spanish and some indigenous languages. It's pronounced as *nee*. You'll see more examples of this later in this book.

- O, pronounced as the letter *a* when it appears in the word *all*.

- P, pronounced as it appears in *potatoes*.

- Q, only used in combination with the letters *ue* or *ui*, forming *que* and *qui*. Their pronunciations are like *ke* when it appears in *keto,* and *ki* when it appears in *Kim*.

- R, pronounced as it appears in *Russian*.

- S, pronounced as it appears in *Susan*.

- T, pronounced as it appears in *Timmy*.

- U, pronounced as *oo* when it appears in words like *boot* and *room.*

- V, pronounced as it appears in *vacation* and *Vermont.*

- W, pronounced as it appears in *what, where,* and *water.*

- X, pronounced as it appears, in *example.*

- Y, pronounced as it appears in *yes* (The letters *ll* and *y* have very similar pronunciations in Spanish). Also, pronounced as *ee* as it appears in *need* **only** when it's used as the equivalent of the English word *and.*

- Z, pronounced as it appears in *zebra.*

Pronunciation

You'll see how some Spanish words are pronounced in this book. Many of the letters in the alphabet have clear pronunciations, let's see some examples:

Spanish Word	Pronunciation	Translation
árbol	ahr-bohl	tree
bebé	beh-beh	baby
comer	koh-mehr	eat
duele	doo-eh-leh	hurts
enemigo	eh-neh-mee-goh	enemy
familia	fah-mee-lee-ah	family
ganar	gah-nahr	win

hombre	ohm-breh	man
Chile	chee-leh	Chile
alcohol	ahl-koh-ohl	alcohol
imán	ee-mahn	magnet
jugar	hoo-ghar	play
jinete	hee-neh-teh	horse rider
kilo	kee-loh	kilo
luna	loo-nah	moon
Madrid	mah-dreed	Madrid
nada	nah-dah	nothing
ola	oh-lah	wave
pequeño	peh-keh-nee-oh	little/small
quemar	keh-mahr	burn
ratón	rah-tohn	mouse
salir	sah-leer	go out
todo	toh-doh	all/everything
usar	oo-sahr	use
vaca	vah-kah	cow
w		
éxito	ek-see-toh	success
yema	yeh-mah	egg yolk
zapato	zah-pah-toh	shoe

Articles

Spanish has indefinite and definite articles. Let's see the indefinite articles:

Indefinite Articles			
Singular		**Plural**	
Masculin	Feminine	Masculin	Feminine
Un	Una	Unos	Unas
English: A		**Some**	

As the name implies, you can use these indefinite articles when you don't know exactly the number of objects or people you're talking about. Spanish differentiates between masculine and feminine nouns, and the articles have to correspond to the gender being used. Let's see some examples:

Un amigo	A friend
Un árbol	A tree
Un celular	A cell phone
Un corazón	A heart

Una amiga	A friend
Una computadora	A car
Una televisión	A TV
Una palabra	A word

Unos amigos	some friends
unos árboles	some trees
unos corazones	some hearts

unas amigas	some friends
unas radios	some radios
unas llamadas	some calls

Now let's see the definite articles:

Definite Articles			
Singular		**Plural**	
Masculin	Feminine	Masculin	Feminine
El	la	los	las
English: The		**The**	

Let's see some examples of definite articles being used:

El perrito	the puppy
el trineo	the sleigh

Los perros	the dogs
los carros	the cars

la mamá	the mother
la puerta	the door

| las puertas | the doors |
| las sandalias | the sandals |

In Spanish, nouns can be either masculine or feminine. You need to use definite or indefinite articles that correspond to the noun's gender.

Colors

Spanish has its own way to name the different spectrum of colors. Let's see some of them:

Spanish
1. rojo
2. celeste
3. marrón
4. verde
5. morado
6. rosado

7. negro
8. gris
9. amarillo
10. blanco
11. azul

English
1. red
2. light blue
3. brown
4. green
5. purple
6. pink
7. black
8. gray
9. yellow
10. white
11. blue

All of the colors can also be used as adjectives. Let's see how you can use adjectives and nouns together.

Adjectives

Unlike English, Spanish adjectives are usually placed after the noun. Also, since nouns can be either feminine or masculine, adjectives also need to adjust their gender to the respective noun's gender. What are the most common articles?

Spanish				English
Singular		Plural		
Masculine	Feminine	Masculine	Feminine	
alto	alta	altos	altas	tall
gordo	gorda	gordos	gordas	fat
bajo	baja	bajos	bajas	short
inteligente	inteligente	inteligentes	inteligentes	smart
malo	mala	malos	malas	bad
flaco	flaca	flacos	flacas	thin
ruidoso	ruidosa	ruidosos	ruidosas	noisy
asustado	asustada	asustados	asustadas	afraid
feliz	feliz	felices	felices	happy
fuerte	fuerte	fuertes	fuertes	strong
triste	triste	triste	triste	sad
bonito	bonita	bonitos	bonitas	beautiful
joven	joven	jóvenes	jóvenes	young
bueno	Buena	Buenos	buenas	good
viejo	vieja	viejos	Viejas	old
aburrido	aburrida	aburridos	aburridas	bored
amable	amable	amables	amables	kind
caliente	caliente	calientes	calientes	hot
largo	larga	largos	largas	long
dulce	dulce	dulces	dulces	sweet
enojado	enojada	enojados	enojadas	angry

feo	fea	feos	feas	ugly
grande	grande	grandes	grandes	big
lento	lenta	lentos	lentas	slow
tímido	tímida	tímidos	tímidas	shy

Having in mind the colors, you can also see how they can be used as adjectives:

Spanish				English
Singular		Plural		
Masculine	Feminine	Masculine	Feminine	
rojo	rojas	rojos	rojas	red
verde	verde	verdes	verdes	green
amarillo	amarilla	amarillos	amarillas	yellow
rosado	rosada	rosados	rosadas	pink
blanco	blanca	blancos	blancas	white
azul	azul	azules	azules	blue
celeste	celeste	celestes	celestes	light blue
marrón	marrón	marrones	marrones	brown
negro	negra	negros	negras	black
gris	gris	grises	grises	gray
morado	morada	morados	moradas	purple

As you may have noticed, adjectives that are in bold don't need any additional change to conform to the noun's gender. In other words, they can be used with either masculine or feminine nouns. A word of caution, though: if these adjectives are used in their plural form, they still need to be added the termination **–s** or **-es.** Plural nouns and adjectives are usually formed by adding **–s** or **–es.**

As you may have also noticed, these special adjectives usually end in **e** (*inteligente, fuerte, triste, celeste, amable, caliente, dulce, grande*) or end in a consonant (*feliz, joven, azul, marrón, gris*). In the case of adjectives that end in **z,** you need to replace the letter **z** with **c** and then add **–es** to form their plural forms (*feliz/felices*)

Let's see some examples of these adjectives in use

Caja roja	red box
casa grande	big house
gata bonita	beautiful cat
regla larga	long rule

amigo alto	tall friend
perro grande	big dog
profesor inteligente	smart teacher
cielo azul	blue sky

perros gordos	fat dogs
libros morados	purple books
hombres jóvenes	young men
niños tímidos	shy children

zapatillas blancas	white snickers

tortugas lentas	slow turtles
clases aburridas	boring classes
personas enojadas	angry people

Adjectives can also be used as adverbs. Let's see some of them in the next section.

Adverbs

While adjectives modify and qualify nouns, adverbs do the same but to adjectives and also verbs. As a rule of thumb, if the adverb is modifying a verb, then it will appear after the verb; and if it's modifying an adjective, it will appear before the adjective.

Adjectives can usually turn into adverbs if you add the termination **–mente.** Let's see some of the most popular adverbs.

Spanish Adjectives	Spanish Adverbs	English
rápido	rápidamente	fastly
lento	lentamente	slowly
fácil	fácilmente	easily
difícil	difícilmente	with difficulty
ruidoso	ruidosamente	noisily
perfecto	perfectamente	perfectly
dulce	dulcemente	sweetly

Here's how they are usually used:

Spanish	English
Él come rápidamente	He eats fastly
Él canta facilmente	He sings easily
Ella hace la tarea perfectamente	She does her homework perfectly
Ella habla dulcemente	She speaks sweetly
Ellos juegan ruidosamente	They play noisily

Adverbs of frequency also exist in Spanish:

Spanish
1. una vez a la semana
2. siempre
3. a veces
4. nunca
5. casi nunca
6. a menudo
7. dos veces a la semana
8. en los fines de semana
9. una vez al mes
10. todos los días
11. de vez en cuando
12. ayer
13. hoy

14. mañana
15. ahora
16. anoche
17. pasado mañana
18. anteayer
19. temprano
20.tarde

English
1. once a week
2. always
3. sometimes
4. never
5. hardly ever
6. often
7. twice a week
8. on the weekends
9. once a month
10. everyday
11. from time to time
12. yesterday
13. today
14. tomorrow
15. now

16. last night
17. the day after tomorrow
18. the day before yesterday
19. early
20. late

Let's see how these are used:

Spanish	English
Yo siempre hago mi tarea	I always do my homework
Él nunca limpia su habitación	He never cleans his room
Mis padres llegaron ayer	My parents arrived yesterday
Terminé mi tarea anoche	I finished my homework last night
Voy al gimnasio todos los días con mis amigos después de clases	I go to the gym every day with my friends after school

If you want to talk about places, you can use the following adverbs of place:

Spanish	English
Aquí	here
Acá	Here

allá	there
Allí	there
delante	in front of
detrás	behind
arriba	above
abajo	below
sobre	on
dentro	in/inside
debajo	under
en medio de	between
al costado de	next to
fuera	outside
cerca	near
lejos	far

Let's see how some of these adverbs of place are used:

Spanish	English
Estamos cerca del aeropuerto	We're near the airport
Ellos están aquí	They're here
Mis amigos están afuera de mi casa	My friends are outside my house
Mi pelota está debajo de mi cama	My ball is under my bed

There are also adverbs of quality. These adverbs can be used with verbs, adjectives and adverbs alike. Let's see some of them:

Spanish	English
Muy	very
demasiado	too much
tanto	so much
mucho	a lot
menos	less
más	more
poco	a little
nada	nothing/ not at all
bastante/suficeiente	enough

Here's how some of them are used:

Spanish	English
Ellos comen muy rapido	They eat very fast
Mi hermana escribe muy lentamente	My sister writes very slowly
No hizo nada	He didn't do anything
Mi tía está muy cansada	My aunt is very tired
La fiesta está un poco aburrida	The party is a little boring
Hay demasiada comida	There's too much food

There are also some adverbial expressions that are used to convey the way in which something has been done:

English	Spanish	
	Adverbial expression	Adverb/Origin
blindly	a ciegas	ciegamente. From *ciego (blind)*
finally	por fin	finalmente
in the end	al final	
carelessly	sin ciudado	descuidadamente
carefully	con cuidado	cuidadosamente
perfectly	a la perfección	perfectamente
immediately	de inmediato	inmediatamente
actually	en realidad	
once again	de nuevo	nuevamente
really	en serio	seriamente
secretly	a escondidas	escondidamente
happily	con alegría	alegremente
sadly	con tristeza	tristemente
suddenly	de repente	repentinamente
suddenly	de pronto	
unfortunately	por desgracias	desgraciadamente

In order to better understand the adverbs, you need to learn the Spanish personal pronouns and also the verbs.

You'll see this in Chapter. In the meantime, you can see how you can tell the time in Spanish in the following section.

Time and Numbers

Telling time in Spanis is simpler than you think. To begin, you first need to learn the numbers in Spanish.

Spanish
0. cero
1. uno
2. dos
3. tres
4. cuatro
5. cinco
6. seis
7. siete
8. ocho

9. nueve
10. diez
11. once
12. doce
13. trece
14. catorce
15. quince
16. dieciseis
17. diecisiete
18. dieciocho
19. diecinueve
20. veinte
21. veintiuno
22. veintidos
23. veintitres
24. veinticuatro

English
0. zero
1. one
2. two
3. three
4. four
5. five

6.	six
7.	seven
8.	eight
9.	nine
10.	ten
11.	eleven
12.	twelve
13.	thirteen
14.	fourteen
15.	fifteen
16.	sixteen
17.	seventeen
18.	eighteen
19.	nineteen
20.	twenty
21.	twenty-one
22.	twenty-two
23.	twenty-three
24.	twenty-four

Now let's see how time is expressed in Spanish:

- *En punto – O'clock*

1.	Es la una en punto
2.	Son las ocho en punto

3. Son las dos en punto
4. Son las cinco en punto

1. It's one o'clock
2. It's eight o'clock
3. It's two o'clock
4. It's five o'clock

You need to first begin the sentence with *Es* if the time is one. If it's any other time, you have to use *Son,* which is the plural form of *Es*. Both can be translated into English as *It's*.

1. Son las 12 en punto
2. Son las 9 en punto
3. Son las 3 en punto

1. It's 12 o'clock
2. It's 9 o'clock
3. It's 3 o'clock

- *Un cuarto pasado las... - A quarter after...*

If you want to say that 15 minutes have passed since the top of the hour, you can use the expression *Un cuarto pasado la...* if it's 15 minutes after one; you can use *Un cuarto pasado las...* if it's any other time you're talking about (*las* is just the plural form of *las*)

1. Es un cuarto pasado las cinco
2. Es un cuarto pasado las ocho
3. Es un cuarto pasado las 9
4. Es un cuarto pasado las 6
5. Es un cuarto pasado la 1

1. It's a quarter past five
2. It's a quarter past eight
3. It's a quarter past nine
4. It's a quarter past 6
5. It's a quarter past 1

You can also say ... *y cuarto* (*and a quarter*):

1. Son las diez y cuarto
2. Son las 5 y cuarto
3. Son las 8 y cuarto
4. Es la una y cuarto

1. It's a quarter past ten
2. It's a quarter past 5
3. It's a quarter past 8
4. It's a quarter past 1

Finally, you can also choose not to use any of the expressions mentioned above and say... *y quince* (*fifteen*)

1. Son las 3 y quince
2. Son las 11 y quince
3. Son las dos y quince
4. Es la una y quince

1. It's 3 fifteen
2. It's 11 fifteen
3. It's two fifteen
4. It's two fifteen

- *... Y media – Half past*

To say that 30 minutes have passed since the top of the hour, you can use... *y media.*

1. Son las tres y media
2. Son las 5 y media
3. Es la una y media
4. Son las doce y media

1. It's half past 3
2. It's half past 5
3. It's half past one
4. It's half past twelve

If you don't want to use this expression, then you can say
... *y treinta* (*thirty*)

1. Es la una y treinta
2. Son las cinco y treinta
3. Son las 12 y treinta
4. Son las 8 y treinta

1. It's one thirty
2. It's five thirty
3. It's twelve thirty
4. It's 8 thirty

- *Quince para la/las... - A quarter to...*

If you want to say that 45 minutes have passed since the top of the hour, you can use *quince para la/las...*

Son quince para las 4	It's a quarter to 4
Son quince para las cinco	It's a quarter to 5
Son quince para las ocho	It's a quarter to eight
Son quince para las 7	It's a quarter to seven

Just like with the other examples, you can decide not to use this expression and use ... *y cuarenta y cinco* (*...forty-five*)

1. Son las 8 y cuarenta y cinco
2. Son las 9 y cuarenta y cinco
3. Es la una y cuarenta y cinco

4. Son las once y cuarenta y cinco

1. It's eight forty-five
2. It's 9 forty-five
3. It's one forty-five
4. It's eleven forty-five

- *Tiempo de 24 horas – 24 hour time*

You can also use military time. This is not really common in informal settings, but you'll likely see it in the news, on TV, on bills, and on other documents.

Son las 23 y 55	It's 23:55
Son las veintiuno y quince	It's twenty-one fifteen
Son 20 minutos después de las 10	It's twenty minutes after ten
Son las 5 y ocho	It's five eight

- *Otras expresiones de tiempo – Other time expressions*

Spanish
1. En la mañana
2. A la medianoche
3. En la tarde
4. En la madrugada
5. En la noche

English
1. In the morning
2. At midnight
3. In the afternoon
4. In the wee hours
5. At night/In the evening

If you want to tell someone that a certain event will take place at a certain time, you need to say *a la/las... (at...)*

La fiesta será a las 5 en punto	The party will be at 5 o'clock
Mis clases comienzan a las 4 y treinta	My classes begin at 4 thirty
Llegaré a las 8 y cuarto	I'll arrive at a quarter past eight
Ella llamará a las 8 en punto	She'll call at 8 o'clock

If you want to say that a certain event will happen some time later, like in 5 minutes or in some hours, you can say:

Llamaré en 5 minutos	I'll call in 5 minutes
Llamaré dentro de 5 minutos	I'll call within 5 minutes

Llegaré en cinco horas	I'll arrive in five hours

Llegaré en dos horas	I'll arrive in two hours

- *Los meses – Months*

Spanish
1. Enero
2. febrero
3. marzo
4. abril
5. mayo
6. junio
7. julio
8. agosto
9. setiembre
10. octubre
11. noviembre
12. diciembre

And this is the translation of the words listed above:

English
1. January
2. February
3. March
4. April
5. may

6. June	
7. July	
8. August	
9. September	
10. October	
11. November	
12. December	

As you can see, months in Spanish don't need to have their first letters capitalized.

To say that a certain event is going to take place on a certain day of the month, you might say:

El 3 de agosto	August 3
El 8 de mayo	May 8
El 15 de febrero	February 15
El 3 de abril	April 3

La fiesta será el 4 de agosto	The party will be on the fourth of August
Mi mamá llegará el 14 de diciembre	My mom will arrive on December the fourteenth
Mis clases acabarán el 15 de junio	My classes will finish on June 15
Mi amigo me visitará el 20 marzo	My friend will visit me on March 20

- *Los días de la semana – Days of the week*

Spanish
1. lunes
2. martes
3. miércoles
4. jueves
5. viernes
6. sábado
7. domingo

And this is the translation

English
1. Monday
2. Tuesday
3. Wednesday
4. Thursday
5. Friday
6. Saturday
7. Sunday

As you can also see here, the names of the days in Spanish don't have their first letters capitalized. Let's see some expressions that are used with the days of the week:

El siguiente sábado	Next Saturday

El sábado pasado	Last Saturday
El siguiente lunes	Next Monday
El juevcs pasado	Last Thursday
El lunes por la mañana	Monday morning
El primero domingo del mes	The first Sunday of the month
El último domingo del mes	The last Sunday of the month
El domingo por la noche	Sunday night
El martes por la tarde	Tuesday afternoon
El viernes por la noche	Friday night

- *Los años – Years*

You might need to know how to count up to the thousands to get the right year. Here you will see how people use the years in conversations and documents:

Year	Spanish	Important Event
1347	Mil trecientos cuarenta y siete	Año de la llegada de la peste negra a Europa
1492	Mil cuatrocientos noventa y dos	Año del descubrimiento de América
1776	Mil setecientos setenta y seis	Año de la independencia de los Estados Unidos
1914	Mil novecientos catorce	Año en que empezó la primera guerra mundial

251

1945	Mil novecientos cuarenta y cinco	Año en que la segunda guerra mundial finalizó
2007	Dos mil siete	Año del lanzamiento del primero iPhone
2004	Dos mil cuatro	Año del lanzamiento de Facebook
2016	Dos mil 2016	Año del referéndum sobre Brexit

Now let's see the translation of the important events:

1347	Año de la llegada de la peste negra a Europa	The Black Death reaches Europe
1492	Año del descubrimiento de América	Discovery of America
1776	Año de la independencia de los Estados Unidos	Independence of the United States
1914	Año en que empezó la primera guerra mundial	Beginning of the first World War
1945	Año en que la segunda guerra mundial finalizó	End of World War II
2007	Año del lanzamiento del primero iPhone	Release of the first iPhone
2004	Año del lanzamiento de Facebook	Launch of Facebook

| 2016 | Año del referéndum sobre Brexit | Brexit referendum |

Now let's see when these happened exactly:

| El descubrimiento de América ocurrió el 12 de octubre de 1492 |
| The discovery of America occurred on October 12, 1492 |

| Los americanos celebran su independencia el 4 de julio de cada año. |
| Americans celebrate their independence every fourth of July. |

| La segunda guerra terminó el 2 de setiembre de 1945 |
| WWII ended on September 1945 |

| Los británicos votaron el 23 de junio del 2016. |
| British people voted on June 23, 2016 |

- *Las décadas y los siglos – Decades and centuries*

The decades are counted in tens, and the centuries are counted in hundreds. How do you count them both in Spanish?

| La primera década del 2000 | The first decade of the 2000s |

La última década de este siglo	The last decade of this century
Ocurrieron muchas cosas en la anterior década	Many things occurred in the last decade

El siglo XX	The 20th century
El siglo XVIII	The 18th century
El siglo XXI	The 21st century

As you may have noticed, centuries in Spanish are written in Roman numerals, but they are expressed in cardinal numbers (twenty, dieciocho, veintiuno)

Where can you find all of what you have learned in a sentence? While it's pretty hard to find them in a simple conversation, you will definitely find them in any important documents and you'll possibly hear it from an experienced teacher:

La conocí el domingo, 4 de octubre del 2018 a las 3:30 de la tarde
I met her on Sunday, October 4, 2018, at 3:30 in the afternoon.

Mi hermana me llamó el domingo pasado a las 5 y cuarto.
My sister called me last Sunday at a quarter past 5.

La cita con mi novio será el 8 de diciembre a las 2 en punto.
The date with my boyfriend will be on December 8 at 2 o'clock

Prepositions and Conjunctions

Prepositions are terms that help us understand the relation between certain words. They can express many things: origin, direction, motive and more.

Let's see the most popular prepositions:

- A, which can express direction, time and manner

A	To
Iré a tu casa.	
I'll go to your house	

- Ante, which expresses location

Ante	Before
El profesor estaba ante mí	
The teacher was in front of me	

- Bajo, which expresses location and manner

Bajo	Under
Estoy trabajando bajo su dirección	I'm working under his direction
El cuaderno esta bajo la cama de tu hermano menor	The notebook is under your younger brother's bed

- Con, which expresses company

Con	With
Estoy caminando con mi esposa	
I'm walking with my wife	

- De, which expresses, origin, manner, content and more

De	Of/From
Yo vengo de Lima	I come from Lima
Esto es de Mariana	This belongs to Mariana
Esta es la clase de matemáticas	This is math class

- Desde, which expresses time and origin

Desde	Since/From
Estaremos esperando por ti desde las 8 de la noche	We'll be waiting for you since 8 in the evening

¿Puedes verme desde allí?	Can you see me from over there?

- Durante, wich expresses time

Durante	During
Ellos bailarán durante toda la noche	
They will dance all night	

- En, which expresses location

En	In
Yo estoy en el cine	
I'm in the movie theater	

- Entre, which expresses time and location

Entre	Between
El profesor vendrá entre las 3 y las 4	
The teacher will come between 3 and 4	

- Excepto, which expresses exception

Excepto	Except
Me gusta todo excepto el café	
I like everything except coffee	

- Hasta; which expresses direction or limit of time

Hasta	Until

Corrieron hasta el supermercado	They run until the supermarket
Te espere hasta las 10	I waited for you until 10

- Hacia, which expresses direction and time

Hacia	To/Ago
Ella miró hacia el oceano	She gazed at the ocean
Nosotros llegamos hacia tres horas	We arrived 3 hours ago.

- Mediante; which introduces the means by which something is done

Mediante	Through/By means of
Las noticias se anunciaron mediante el teléfono	
The news was announced through the phone	

- Para; which expresses direction, time and purpose

Para	For
Salió para Montecarlo	He left for Montecarlo
Hace su tarea para salir a jugar temprano.	He does his homework to go out to play with his friends.

- Por, which expresses place, purpose, time, means, manner, and more

Por	For
Caminamos por el centro comercial	We walked in the mall
Me llamaran por la noche.	They will call me at night

- Salvo, a synonym of *excepto,* it also expresses exception

Salvo	Except/Bar
Llamé a todos salvo María	
I call everyone except Maria	

- Según, which expresses the manner

Según	according to
Según mi profesor, necesitamos estudiar mucho si queremos aprobar	
According to my teacher, we need to study a lo if we want to pass	

- Sin, antonym of *con;* expresses deprivation of something or someone

Sin	Without
Fui a una iglesia que está lejos de mi casa sin mi mochila	

> I went to a church that is far my house without my backpack

- Sobre, which expresses place, time or topic

Sobre	About/On
Estaban hablando sobre ti	They were talking about you
El celular estaba sobre la mesa	The cell phone was on the table

- Tras, which expresses time

Tras	After
Tras haber hecho un berrinche, se calmó	
After throwing a tantrum, he calmed down	

There are many conjunctions in Spanish. These are classified into 2 main categories. Let's see some of them:

1. *Las conjunciones coordinantes*

These conjunctions' main function is to relate two different nouns or ideas. Some of the most common are:

Y	And
Juan y Rodrigo irán a la fiesta	

Juan and Rodrigo will go to the party

O	Or
Ahorra más dinero o no gastes mucho	
Save more money or don't spend a lot	

Ni	Nor /Neither
No me gustó la comida ni las bebidas	
I didn't like the food nor the drinks	

Pero	But
Me habla muy dulcemente pero no puedo creer en él	
He speaks very sweetly but I can't believe in him	

2. *Las conjunciones subordinantes*

The conjunctions are used to introduce a subordinate sentence that helps complement the main sentence. Let's see some of the main ones:

Porque	Because
A ella le gusta venir a mi casa porque a ella le gusta jugar conmigo	
She likes coming to my house because she likes playing with me	

Que	That

Ella ha hablado con el profesor sobre la tarea que ella debió haber hecho la semana pasada	
She talked with the teacher about the homework that she should've done last week.	

Si	If
Si salgo con ustedes, regresaré tarde a mi casa	
If I go out with you, I'll get back home late	

Aunque	Even though/Although
El jugará fútbol aunque le duele la pierna	
He will play soccer even though his leg hurts	

Siempre y cuando	As long as
Iré contigo siempre y cuando tú pagues la cuenta	
I'll go with you as long as you pay for the bill	

Mientras	While
Mientras nosotros cocinamos, ustedes pueden limpiar el comedor	
While we cook, you can clean the dining room	

Structure of Sentences

Spanish has a very similar way to build sentences as English. Spanish sentences are divided into two main parts:

- *El sujeto*

El sujeto is usually the first part of the sentence. Inside *el sujeto* you'll find :

1. *El sustantivo – Noun*

Here you'll find the personal pronouns and proper names of people, places, and organizations

2. *Los modificadores – Modifiers*

These modifiers include adjectives, articles and even some adverbs. Some modifiers need prepositions to work; these types of modifiers are called *indirect modifiers.*

- *El Predicado*

El predicado is usally found after *el sujeto.* Inside *el predicado,* you'll find:

1. *El objeto directo – the direct object*

If the verb's action "falls" or is received directly by a thing or person, then it's an indirect object.

2. *El objeto indirecto – the indirect object*

Conversely, if an object or person gets the benefit or damage from a verb's action, then it's an indirect object.

3. *El complemento cirsunstancial* – *The Circumstantial complement*

As its name says, the circumstantial complement complements the sentence with more information about the location, time and more. It provides information about the circumstances of the action.

4. *El verbo* – *The verb*

The most important part of *el predicado* is the verb. The verb transmits the action and what the noun is doing.

Will you usually find all of these in a sentence? Possibly. While it's important to know all about the structure of sentences in Spanish, it's also important to remember that not all of its parts will appear in one sentence most of the time.

Let's see some examples:

1. El perro rojo fue al parque del centro de le ciudad				
El	Perro	Rojo	fue	al parque del centro de la ciudad

Modificador (Artículo)	Sujeto	Modificador (Adjetivo)	Verbo	Complemento circunstancial
Modifier (Article)	Noun	Modifier (Adjective)	Verb	Circumstantial complement

2. El muchacho alto dio una carta a María					
El	muchacho	alto	dio	una carta	a María
Modificador (Artículo)	Sujeto	Modificador (Adjetivo)	Verbo	Objeto directo	Objeto indirecto
Modifier (Article)	Noun	Modifier (Adjective)	Verb	Direct object	Indirect object

3. Mi hermano mayor está en la escuela				
Mi	hermano	mayor	está	en la escuela
Modificador (Artículo)	Sujeto	Modificador (Adjetivo)	Verbo	Complemento circunstancial
Modifier (Article)	Noun	Modifier (Adjective)	Verb	Circumstantial complement

This is the translation of the sentences:

1. El perro rojo fue al parque del centro de le ciudad

The red dog went to the park in the city center

2. El muchacho alto dio una carta a María

The tall guy gave Maria a letter

3. Mi hermano mayor está en la escuela

My older brother is at school

At this point, you already know how some sentences are formed and how they work. There might be some terms that you still don't understand, but that's fine. Your doubts will be cleared in the following chapters.

One of the most important parts of the sentences is the noun. In the following chapter, you'll learn more about it and how you can benefit from learning when and how to use it.

Exercises

I. Use the **definite** article that corresponds to the noun:

1. _ amiga de Juan

2. _ perro de Roberto

3. No encuentro _ libros del profesor

4. Estoy escuchando _ radio

5. ¿Quién está lavando _ platos?

II. Use the **indefinite** article that corresponds to the noun:

1. Estoy leyendo _ libro

2. ¿Quién tiene _ moneda que pueda prestarme?

3. Tenemos _ amiga viviendo en Montreal.

4. Hay que usar _ cable para conctarlo.

5. Mi amigo tiene _ perro y _ gata.

III. Complete the translation of the colors:

1. rojo –

2. yellow –

3. rosado –

4. black –

5. blanco –

6. marrón –

7. morado –

8. gray –

9. green –

IV. Write the adjective you wish for the noun:

1. Ella es una mujer _

2. Hubo un ruido muy fuerte. Yo estaba _

3. Me siento muy _ de volver a verte

4. Él puede levantar hasta 200 kilogramos. Él es muy _

5. Creo que él está _. Escuché que su perrito murió ayer.

6. Tu mamá es muy _. Ella me ayudo con mi tarea.

7. Este río es _. No lo podremos cruzar.

8. Él está _. No está prestando atención a la clase.

V. Write what time it is in Spanish:

1. 3:15

2. 8:30

3. 9:00

4. 6:45

5. 8:15

VI. Try to tell time what it is:

1. La una y cuarto

2. las cinco y media

3. un cuarto pasado las dos

4. quince para las 9

5. las ocho en punto

VII. Complete the translation of the days and months of the year:

1. lunes

2. noviembre

3. jueves

4. domingo

5. enero

6. diciembre

7. martes

8. febrero

9. octubre

10. agosto

11. sábado

Chapter 2: Grammar

Personal Pronouns

You don't have to worry too much about the number of personal pronouns in Spanish. They are just one more than English.

Yo	1st person	Singular	I
Tú	2nd person		You
Él	3rd person		He/It
Ella			She/It
Nosotros	1st person	Plural	We
Ustedes/Vosotros	2nd person		You
Ellos/Ellas	3rd person		They

The additional personal pronoun is *ustedes*. This is the plural form of *tú (you)*. You can also see that there's another personal pronoun next to it. *Vosotros* is the same as *ustedes*; the only difference being that *vosotros* is mostly used in Spain, Argentina, Uruguay and some parts of the Andes. You will also find it in ancient literature and as polite speech.

You may have also noticed that the personal pronoun *ellos*

Personal pronouns, of course, need verbs to function properly. The verbs *ser* and *estar (be)*.The most well-known verbs are, of course,

The verbs Ser and Estar

The verb *ser* is conjugated as follows:

1.	Yo soy
2.	Tú eres
3.	Él es
4.	Ella es
5.	Nosotros somos
6.	Ustedes son
7.	Vosotros sois
8.	Ellos/Ellas son

1.	I am
2.	You are
3.	He is
4.	She is
5.	We are
6.	You are
7.	You are
8.	They are

The verb *ser* usually conveys permanence, origin, quality, identity and even possession. Let's see some examples where *ser* is used.

Mi hermano es francés
My brother is French

Nosotros somos los mejores de la clase
We're the best in the class

Yo soy muy inteligente
I'm very intelligent

La computadora es mía
The computer is mine

If you want to form negative sentences with the verb *ser*, you just need to place *no* before the conjugation of the verb *be*. Let's see some examples:

Mi hermano no es francés
My brother is not French

Nosotros no somos los mejores de la clase
We're not the best in the class

Yo no soy muy inteligente
I'm not very intelligent

| La computadora no es mía |
| The computer is not mine |

The verb *ser* can also be used without personal pronouns. That's a special feature of verbs and personal pronouns in Spanish. A sentence doesn't really need a personal pronoun or, in some cases, a noun to be understood. This is because the conjugation of the verb – any verb – carries enough information about the noun or personal pronoun that's using it. When the noun doesn't appear in the sentence, it's called *sujeto tácito*

Let's see some examples of this with the verb *ser*

| Es muy tarde. |
| It's too late |

| Son jugadores profesionales de fútbol |
| They're professional soccer players |

| Somos mejores amigos |
| We're the best friends |

The verb to be in Spanish has also another meaning: the verb *estar*

The verb *estar* is conjugated as follows:

Yo estoy
Tú estás
Él está
Ella está
Nosotros estamos
Ustedes están
Vosotros estáis
Ellos/Ellas están

I am
You are
He is
She is
We are
You are
You are
They are

The verb *estar* conveys emotion, aspect, location, price and more.

This verb is also used to form the gerund.

Let's see some examples of the verb *estar*

Mis amigos están en la escuela
My friends are at school

Mis amigos y yo estamos en el hospital.
We're in the hospital

Tu mamá está muy contenta por las noticias
Your mom is very happy for the news

If you want to form negative sentences with the verb *estar*, you can place the *no* before the right conjugation of the verb *estar:*

Mis amigos no están en la escuela
My friends are not at school

Nosotros no estamos en el hospital
We're not in the hospital

Tu mamá no está muy contenta por las noticias
Your mom is not very happy for the news

Just like all other verbs, the verb *estar* can be "used" with the verb *estar*

Estoy muy enfermo
I'm very sick

Están jugando fútbol conmigo
They're playing soccer with me

Estamos preparados para la tormenta
We're ready for the storm

Está cerca de la escuela
She's near the school

Of course, there are more than just two verbs in the Spanish vocabulary. While there are hundreds of verbs in Spanish, you can learn the most important and used by native speakers on a daily basis. Which ones are they?

Other Verbs

All of the verbs shown here will be conjugated in the present, past and future tense. Their gerund form will be shown if it exists.

Some important verbs you need to learn are:

The verb **abrir** *(open)*						
	Yo	Tú	Él/Ella	Nosotros	Ustedes	Ellos
Present	abro	abres	abre	abrimos	abren	abren
Past	abrí	abriste	abrió	abrimos	abrieron	abrieron
Future	abriré	abrirás	abrirá	abriremos	abrirán	abrirán
Gerund	abriendo					

The verb **acabar** (finish/end)

	Yo	Tú	Él/Ella	Nosotros	Ustedes	Ellos
Present	acabo	acabas	acaba	acabamos	acabam	acaban
Past	acabé	acabaste	acabó	acabamos	acabaron	acabaron
Future	acabaré	acabarás	acabará	acabaremos	acabarán	acabarán
Gerund	acabiendo					

The verb **aceptar** (accept)

	Yo	Tú	Él/Ella	Nosotros	Ustedes	Ellos
Present	acepto	aceptas	acepta	aceptamos	aceptan	aceptan
Past	acepté	aceptaste	aceptó	aceptamos	aceptaron	aceptaron
Future	aceptaré	aceptarás	aceptará	aceptaremos	aceptarán	aceptarán
Gerund	aceptando					

The verb **cambiar** (change)

	Yo	Tú	Él/Ella	Nosotros	Ustedes	Ellos
Present	cambio	cambias	cambia	cambiamos	cambian	cambian
Past	cambié	cambiaste	cambió	cambiamos	cambiaron	cambiaron
Future	cambiaré	cambiarás	cambiará	cambiaremos	cambiarán	cambiarán
Gerund	cambiando					

The verb **ayudar** (help)

	Yo	Tú	Él/Ella	Nosotros	Ustedes	Ellos
Present	ayudo	ayudas	ayuda	ayudamos	ayudan	ayudan
Past	ayudé	ayudaste	ayudó	ayudamos	ayudaron	ayudaron

	ayudaré	ayudarás	ayudará	ayudaremos	ayudarán	ayudarán
Future						
Gerund	ayudando					

The verb **buscar** *(search/look for)*

	Yo	Tú	Él/Ella	Nosotros	Ustedes	Ellos
Present	busco	buscas	busca	buscamos	buscan	buscan
Past	busqué	buscaste	buscó	buscamos	buscaron	buscaron
Future	buscaré	buscarás	buscará	buscaremos	buscarán	buscarán
Gerund	buscando					

The verb **comenzar** *(begim/start)*

	Yo	Tú	Él/Ella	Nosotros	Ustedes	Ellos
Present	comienzo	comienzas	comienza	comenzamos	comienzan	comienzan
Past	comencé	comenzaste	comenzó	comenzamos	comenzaron	comenzaron
Future	comenzaré	comenzarás	comenzará	comenzaremos	comenzarán	comenzarán
Gerund	comenzando					

The verb **conocer** *(know/meet)*

	Yo	Tú	Él/Ella	Nosotros	Ustedes	Ellos
Present	conozco	conoces	conoce	conocemos	conocen	conocen
Past	conocí	conociste	conoció	conocimos	conocieron	conocieron
Future	conoceré	conocerás	conocerá	conoceremos	conocerán	conocerán
Gerund	conociendo					

The verb **contar** *(count)*

	Yo	Tú	Él/Ella	Nosotros	Ustedes	Ellos
Present	cuento	cuentas	cuenta	contamos	cuentan	cuentan
Past	conté	contaste	contó	contamos	contaron	contaron

278

Future	contaré	contarás	contará	contaremos	contarán	contarán
Gerund	contando					

The verb *correr* (run)

	Yo	Tú	Él/Ella	Nosotros	Ustedes	Ellos
Present	corro	corres	corre	corremos	corren	corren
Past	corrí	corriste	corrió	corrimos	corrieron	corrieron
Future	correré	correrás	correrá	correremos	correrán	correrán
Gerund	corriendo					

The verb *dar* (give)

	Yo	Tú	Él/Ella	Nosotros	Ustedes	Ellos
Present	doy	das	da	damos	dan	dan
Past	di	diste	dio	dimos	dieron	dieron
Future	daré	darás	dará	daremos	darán	darán
Gerund	dando					

The verb *encontrar* (find)

	Yo	Tú	Él/Ella	Nosotros	Ustedes	Ellos
Present	encuentro	encuentras	encuentra	encontramos	encuentran	encuentran
Past	encontré	encontraste	encontró	encontramos	encontraron	encontraron
Future	encontraré	encontrarás	encontrará	encontraremos	encontrarán	encontrarán
Gerund	encontrando					

279

The verb *entender* (understand)

	Yo	Tú	Él/Ella	Nosotros	Ustedes	Ellos
Present	entiendo	entendiste	entiende	entendemos	entienden	entienden
Past	entendí	entendiste	entendió	entendimos	entendieron	entendieron
Future	entenderé	entenderás	entenderá	entenderemos	entenderán	entenderán
Gerund	entendiendo					

The verb *entrar* (enter)

	Yo	Tú	Él/Ella	Nosotros	Ustedes	Ellos
Present	entro	entras	entra	entramos	entran	entran
Past	entré	entraste	entró	entramos	entraron	entraron
Future	entraré	entrarás	entrará	entraremos	entrarán	entrarán
Gerund	entrando					

The verb *escribir* (write)

	Yo	Tú	Él/Ella	Nosotros	Ustedes	Ellos
Present	escribo	escribes	escribe	escribimos	escriben	escriben
Past	escribí	escribiste	escribió	escribimos	escribieron	escribieron
Future	escribiré	escribirás	escribirá	escribiremos	escribirán	escribirán
Gerund	escribiendo					

The verb **estudiar** (study)

	Yo	Tú	Él/Ella	Nosotros	Ustedes	Ellos
Present	estudio	estudias	estudia	estudiamos	estudian	estudian
Past	estudié	estudiaste	estudió	estudiamos	estudiaron	estudiaron
Future	estudiaré	estudiarás	estudiará	estudiarems	estudiarán	estudiarán
Gerund	estudiando					

The verb **hablar** (speak)

	Yo	Tú	Él/Ella	Nosotros	Ustedes	Ellos
Present	hablo	hablas	habla	hablamos	hablan	hablan
Past	hablé	hablaste	habló	hablamos	hablaron	hablaron
Future	hablaré	hablarás	hablará	hablaremos	hablarán	hablarán
Gerund	hablando					

The verb **hacer** (do)

	Yo	Tú	Él/Ella	Nosotros	Ustedes	Ellos
Present	hago	haces	hace	hacemos	hacen	hacen
Past	hice	hiciste	hizo	hicimos	hicieron	hicieron
Future	hare	harás	hare	haremos	harán	harán
Gerund	haciendo					

The verb **ir** (go)

	Yo	Tú	Él/Ella	Nosotros	Ustedes	Ellos
Present	voy	vas	va	vamos	van	van
Past	fui	fuiste	fue	fuimos	fueron	fueron
Future	iré	irás	irá	iremos	irán	irán

Gerund	yendo					

The verb *jugar* (play)

	Yo	Tú	Él/Ella	Nosotros	Ustedes	Ellos
Present	juego	juegas	juega	jugamos	juegan	juegan
Past	jugué	jugaste	jugó	jugamos	jugaron	jugaron
Future	jugaré	jugarás	jugará	jugaremos	jugarán	jugarán
Gerund	jugando					

The verb *leer* (read)

	Yo	Tú	Él/Ella	Nosotros	Ustedes	Ellos
Present	leo	lees	lee	leemos	leen	leen
Past	leí	leíste	leyó	leímos	leyeron	leyeron
Future	leeré	leerás	leerá	leeremos	leerán	leerán
Gerund	leyendo					

The verb *llamar* (call)

	Yo	Tú	Él/Ella	Nosotros	Ustedes	Ellos
Present	llamo	llamas	llama	llamamos	llaman	llaman
Past	llamé	llamaste	llamó	llamamos	llamaron	llamaron
Future	llamaré	llamarás	llamará	llamaremos	llamarán	llamarán
Gerund	llamando					

The verb *mirar* (look at/watch)

	Yo	Tú	Él/Ella	Nosotros	Ustedes	Ellos
Present	miro	miras	mira	miramos	miran	miran
Past	mire	miraste	miró	miramos	miraron	miraron
Future	miraré	mirarás	mirará	miraremos	mirarán	mirarán
Gerund	mirando					

The verb *necesitar* (need)

	Yo	Tú	Él/Ella	Nosotros	Ustedes	Ellos
Present	necesito	necesitas	necesita	necesitamos	necesitan	necesitan

282

Past	necesité	necesitaste	necesitó	necesitamos	necesitaron	necesitaron
Future	necesitaré	necesitarás	necesitará	necesitaremos	necesitarán	necesitarán
Gerund	necesitando					

The verb *oír* (hear)

	Yo	Tú	Él/Ella	Nosotros	Ustedes	Ellos
Present	oigo	oyes	oye	oímos	oyen	oyen
Past	oí	oíste	oyó	oímos	oyeron	oyeron
Future	oiré	oirás	oirá	oiremos	oirán	oirán
Gerund	oyendo					

The verb *pagar* (pay)

	Yo	Tú	Él/Ella	Nosotros	Ustedes	Ellos
Present	pago	pagas	paga	pagamos	pagan	pagan
Past	pagué	pagaste	pagó	pagamos	pagaron	pagaron
Future	pagaré	pagarás	pagará	pagaremos	pagarán	pagarán
Gerund	pagando					

The verb *parar* (stop)

	Yo	Tú	Él/Ella	Nosotros	Ustedes	Ellos
Present	paro	paras	para	paramos	paran	paran
Past	paré	paraste	paró	paramos	pararon	pararon
Future	pararé	pararás	parará	pararemos	pararán	pararán
Gerund	parando					

The verb *poder* (can/ be able to)

	Yo	Tú	Él/Ella	Nosotros	Ustedes	Ellos
Present	puedo	puedes	puede	podemos	pueden	pueden
Past	pude	pudiste	pudo	pudimos	pudieron	pudieron
Future	podré	podrás	podrá	podremos	podrán	podrán
Gerund	pudiendo					

The verb **preguntar** (ask)

	Yo	Tú	Él/Ella	Nosotros	Ustedes	Ellos
Present	pregunto	preguntas	pregunta	preguntamos	preguntan	preguntan
Past	preguntaron	preguntaste	preguntó	preguntamos	preguntaron	preguntaron
Future	preguntaré	preguntarás	preguntará	preguntaremos	preguntarán	preguntarán
Gerund	preguntando					

The verb **querer** (want)

	Yo	Tú	Él/Ella	Nosotros	Ustedes	Ellos
Present	quiero	quieres	quiere	queremos	quieren	quieren
Past	quise	quisiste	quiso	quisimos	quisieron	quisieron
Future	querré	querrás	querrá	querremos	querrán	querrán
Gerund	queriendo					

The verb **recordar** (remember)

	Yo	Tú	Él/Ella	Nosotros	Ustedes	Ellos
Present	recuerdo	recuerdas	recuerda	recordamos	recuerdan	recuerdan
Past	recordé	recordaste	recordó	recordamos	recordaron	recordaron
Future	recordaré	recordarás	recordará	recordaremos	recordarán	recordarán
Gerund	recordando					

The verb **saber** (know)

	Yo	Tú	Él/Ella	Nosotros	Ustedes	Ellos
Present	sé	sabes	sabe	sabemos	saben	saben
Past	supe	supiste	supó	supimos	supieron	supieron
Future	sabré	sabras	sabra	sabremos	sabrán	sabrán
Gerund	sabiendo					

The verb **sentir** *(feel)*

	Yo	Tú	Él/Ella	Nosotros	Ustedes	Ellos
Present	seiento	sientes	siente	sentimos	sienten	sienten
Past	sentí	sentiste	sintió	sentimos	sintieron	sintieron
Future	sentiré	sentirás	sentirá	sentiremos	sentirán	sentirán
Gerund	sintiendo					

The verb **ser** *(be)*

	Yo	Tú	Él/Ella	Nosotros	Ustedes	Ellos
Present	soy	eres	es	somos	son	son
Past	fui	fuiste	fuiste	fue	fueron	fueron
Imperfect	**era**	**eras**	**era**	**éramos**	**eran**	**eran**
Future	seré	serás	será	seremos	serán	serán
Gerund	siendo					

The verb **estar** *(be)*

	Yo	Tú	Él/Ella	Nosotros	Ustedes	Ellos
Present	estoy	estás	está	estamos	están	están
Past	estuve	estuviste	estuvo	estuvimos	estuvieron	estuvieron
Imperfect	**estaba**	**estabas**	**estaba**	**estubimos**	**estubieron**	**estubieron**
Future	estaré	estarás	estará	estaremos	estarán	estarán
Gerund	estando					

The verb **tener** *(have)*

	Yo	Tú	Él/Ella	Nosotros	Ustedes	Ellos
Present	tengo	tienes	tiene	tenemoss	tienen	tienen
Past	tuve	tuviste	tuvó	tuvimos	tuvieron	tuvieron
Future	tendré	tendrás	tendrá	tendremos	tendrán	tendrán
Gerund	teniendo					

The verb **trabajar** *(work)*

	Yo	Tú	Él/Ella	Nosotros	Ustedes	Ellos
Present	trabajo	trabajas	trabaja	trabajamos	trabajan	trabajan
Past	trabajé	trabajaste	trabajó	trabajamos	trajaron	trabajaron
Future	trabajaré	trabajarás	trabajará	trabajaremos	trabajarán	trabajarán
Gerund	trabajando					

The verb **usar** *(use)*

	Yo	Tú	Él/Ella	Nosotros	Ustedes	Ellos
Present	uso	usas	usa	usamos	usan	usan
Past	usé	usaste	usó	usamos	usaron	usaron
Future	usaré	usarás	usará	usaremos	usarán	usarán
Gerund	usando					

The verb **venir** *(come)*

	Yo	Tú	Él/Ella	Nosotros	Ustedes	Ellos
Present	vengo	vienes	viene	venimos	vienen	vienen
Past	vine	viniste	vino	vinimos	vinieron	vinieron
Future	vendré	vendrás	vendrá	vendremos	vendrán	vendrán
Gerund	viniendo					

The verb **ver** *(see)*

	Yo	Tú	Él/Ella	Nosotros	Ustedes	Ellos
Present	veo	ves	ve	vemos	ven	ven
Past	vi	viste	vio	vimos	vieron	vieron
Future	veré	verás	verá	veremos	verán	verán
Gerund	viendo					

286

The verb **volver** (come back)						
	Yo	Tú	Él/Ella	Nosotros	Ustedes	Ellos
Present	vuelvo	vuelves	vuelve	volvemos	vuelven	vuelven
Past	volví	volviste	volvió	volvimos	volvieron	volvieron
Future	volveré	volverás	volverá	volveremos	volverán	volverán
Gerund	volviendo					

Some important things to know about Spanish verbs:

- The great majority of verb conjugations with *ustedes* are the same as *ellos*. That makes it easier to remember the conjugations.

- To form the **gerund,** you need to conjugate the verb *estar* and then add the gerund of the verb you want to use. Like this:

Verb **comer** (eat)	
Yo estoy **comiendo**	I'm eating
Tú estás comiendo un delicioso pastel	You are eating a delicious cake
Él está comiendo con sus amigos de escuela	He's eating with his school friends
Nosotros estamos comiendo un plato de ensalada	We are eating a plate of salad
Ustedes están comiendo un platillo que nunca he visto	You are eating a dish that I've never seen

Ellos están comiendo un platillo muy picante	They are eating a very spicy dish

- All the verbs in Spanish have an infinite form. All the verbs are divided into three main groups: verbs that end in **–ar, -er,** and **–ir.**

- Verbs can also be grouped in regular and irregular verbs. Regular verbs are those that don't drastically change when conjugated; therefore, their conjugations can be easily predicted. Irregular verbs are those whose conjugations might have a different form, sometimes even drastically. One good example of an irregular verb is the verb *ir,* which is shown in one of the charts above.

- There are, of course, more than just 4 tenses in Spanish, but these are the most commonly used and the ones that will come in handy when abroad and when trying to have a simple conversation with native speakers.

- In Spanish, there are two ways to express the past tense: *pretérito (preterite)* and *imperfect (imperfect).* What you have seen in the charts above is the preterite form of the verb since it's the most common. If you want to talk about things that you used to do, you can use the imperfect form of the verb. You have seen some examples of these tenses in the charts of the verbs **ser** and **estar.**

- There are some verbs that need other pronouns to work. These types of verbs are called reflexive verbs.

Reflexive verbs:

Sometimes, a verb's action has the only intention to affect the noun that's using it. When that happens, such a verb is called a reflexive verb. For this to happen, these verbs need a **reflexive pronoun.** Let's see all the reflexive pronouns:

Personal pronoun	Reflexive pronoun
Yo	me
Tú	te
Él/ella	se
nosotros	nos
vosotros	os
ustedes	se
ellos	se

In Spanish, there are many verbs that fall into this category. Since reflexive verbs indicate that someone is doing the action for himself, reflexive pronouns always have to correspond to the noun that is using it. The most common reflexive verbs that follow this rule are:

	Yo	Tú	Él/Ella	Nosotros	Ustedes	Ellos
acostarse (lay)	me acuesto	te acuestas	se acuesta	nos acostamos	se acuestan	se acuestan
bañarse (take a bath)	me baño	te bañas	se baña	nos bañamos	se bañan	se bañan
lavarse (wash)	me lavo	te lavas	se lava	nos lavamos	se lavan	se lavan
peinarse (comb the hair)	me peino	te peina	se peina	nos peinamos	se peinan	se peinan
ponerse (put on clothes)	me pongo	te pones	se pone	nos ponemos	se ponen	se ponen
quitarse (take off clothes)	me quito	te quitas	se quita	nos quitamos	se quitan	se quitan
vestirse (get dressed)	me visto	te vistes	se viste	nos vestimos	se visten	se visten
sentarse (sit)	me siento	te sientes	se sienta	nos sentamos	se sientan	se sientan
maquillarse (put on make up)	me maquillo	te maquillas	se maquilla	nos maquillamos	se maquillan	se maquillan

Let's see some sentences where reflexive sentences are used:

Él se está vistiendo
He's getting dressed

Mi hermana se está maquillando ahora mismo.
My sister is putting on make-up.

Nosotros nos hemos sentado aquí
We took a seat here.

If you want to form negative sentences with reflexive verbs, you just have to write *no* before the reflexive pronoun:

Él no se está vistiendo
He's not getting dressed

Mi hermana no se está maquillando ahora mismo.
My sister is not putting on make-up.

Nosotros no nos hemos sentado aquí
We didn't took a seat here.

Have in mind that reflexive verbs have the "reflexive" termination **–se** added to their infinitive forms to indicate that they are reflexive.

Some verbs can be used as reflexive and also as not reflexive. Some verbs can have totally different meaning depending on if it's being used as a reflexive verb or not. Let's take a look at those types of verbs:

ir(se)	reflexive	to get out/leave	Ella se va de la fiesta	She's leaving the party
	not reflexive	go	Mis padres van a la fiesta	My parents go to the party
levantar(se)	reflexive	get up/stand up	Yo me levanto muy temprano todos los días.	I get up very early every day.
	not reflexive	lift	Él está levantando la silla.	He's lifting the chair
poner(se)	reflexive	put clothes on	Mi papá se está poniendo sus nuevos pantalones.	My dad is putting his new pants on.
	not reflexive	put	Pon el cuaderno sobre la mesa, por favor.	Put the notebook on the table, please.
encontrar(se)	reflexive	feel	¿Cómo te encuentras?	How are you? / How do you feel?
	not reflexive	find/meet/run into/ encountered	Encontré este hermoso cuaderno sobre la mesa.	I found this beautiful notebook on the table.
llamar(se)	reflexive	be named/be called	Él se llama Roberto	His name is Roberto
	not reflexive	call/name	¿A qué hora me llamarás?	What time will you call me?

Let's see now in more detail the past tense of verbs in Spanish.

Past Tense

As previously mentioned, there are 2 ways to express the simple past tense in Spanish:

- *El pretérito – The preterite*

It's used to express that the action the verb describes began and finished in the past. It can also be used to signal that one action interrupted another. To do this, you'll need to have the imperfect in the same tense.

The preterite has a very simple conjugation when it comes to regular verbs:

	Yo	Tú	Él	Nosotros	Ustedes	Ellos
Comer	comí	comiste	comió	comimos	comieron	comieron
hablar	hablé	hablaste	habló	hablamos	hablaron	hablaron
trabajar	trabajé	trabajaste	trabajó	trabajamos	trabajaron	trabajaron
mirar	mire	miraste	miró	miramos	miraron	miraron
escuchar	escuché	escuchaste	escuchó	esuchamos	escucharon	escucharon
usar	usé	usaste	usé	usamos	usaron	usaron
preguntar	pregunté	preguntaste	preguntó	preguntamos	preguntaron	preguntaron

Let's see some sentences where the preterite is used:

Yo comí con mi mamá
I ate with my mom

Yo escuché las noticias ayer
I heard the news yesterday

Ellos miraron la película ayer
They watched the movie yesterday

Mis padres trabajaron en esa compañía
My parents worked in that company

Nosostros no usamos la lavadora.
We didn't use the washing machine.

When it comes to irregular verbs, you might need to memorize their conjugations:

	Yo	Tú	Él	Nosotros	Ustedes	Ellos
volver	volví	volviste	volvió	volvimos	volvieron	volvieron
ver	vi	viste	vio	vimos	vieron	vieron
venir	vine	viniste	vino	vinimos	vinieron	vinieron
tener	tuve	tuviste	tuvó	tuvimos	tuvieron	tuvieron
estar	estuve	estuviste	estuvo	estuvimos	estuvieron	estuvieron
ser	fui	fuiste	fuiste	fue	fueron	fueron
sentir	sentí	sentiste	sintió	sentimos	sintieron	sintieron

Let's see some examples of these verbs being used in sentences:

Volví ayer por la tarde
I came back yesterday afternoon

No vi la película la semana pasada

I didn't see the movie yesterday

Yo estuve con mi mamá allí.
I was there with my mom

Ellos tuvieron más oportunidades
They had more opportunities

Now that you've seen more about the preterite, it's time to get into the *imperfect:*

- *El imperfect – The imperfect*

The imperfect is used to describe routines that occurred in the past, or actions that didn't have a concrete beginning or end. It can be translated as *used to.*

Some of the conjugations of some verbs in Spanish in imperfect are:

	Yo	Tú	Él	Nosotros	Ustedes	Ellos
Comer	comía	comías	comía	comíamos	comían	comían
hablar	hablaba	hablabas	hablaba	hablábamos	hablaban	hablaban
trabajar	trabajaba	trabajabas	trabajaba	trabajábamos	trabajaban	trabajaban
mirar	miraban	mirabas	miraba	mirábamos	miraban	miraban
escuchar	escuchaba	escuchabas	escuchaba	escuchábamos	escuchaban	escuchaban
usar	usaba	usabas	usaba	usábamos	usaban	usaban
preguntar	preguntaba	preguntabas	preguntaba	preguntábamos	preguntaban	preguntaban
volver	volvía	volvías	volvía	volvíamos	volvían	volvían
ver	veía	veías	veía	veíamos	veían	veían
venir	venía	venías	venía	veníamos	venían	venían

tener	tenía	tenías	tenía	teníamos	tenían	tenían
estar	estaba	estabas	estaba	estábamos	estaban	estaban
ser	era	eras	era	éramos	eran	eran
sentir	sentía	sentías	sentía	sentíamos	sentían	sentían

Let's see some examples of these imperfect conjugations:

Él iba a la casa de su amigo todas las tardes después de clases
He would go to his friend's house every afternoon after classes. /He used to go to his friend's house every afternoon after classes

Ellos entrenaban muy lejos de aquí
They would train very far from here.

A mi hermana le gustaba jugar con sus amigas
My sister used to like to play with her friends

Mi mamá me daba de comer todas las semanas
My mom would give me food every week/ My mom used to give me food every week

Remember that it was mentioned that the preterite can be used to signal the interruption of one action by another. Let's see some examples:

Mientras él jugaba fútbol, su mamá le llamó
While he **was playing** soccer, his mother called him.

Ellos estaban mirando la televisión cuando el terremoto ocurrió
They were watching the TV when the earthquake occurred.

Justo cuando ellos empezaban a llevarse bien, un nuevo problema tuvo que ocurrir de nuevo
Just when they were starting to get along, a new problem had to occur again.

What about questions? Well, you can follow these tips to identify and also to use questions in Spanish:

- "Invert" the noun and the main verb:

The structure of a typical sentence is:

Sujeto	Verbo	Complemento
Noun	verb	Complement

One way you can form a question is by inverting the order in which the noun and verb appear. This can also be used with the present and future tenses. Like this:

¿	Verbo	Sujeto	Complemento	?
	verb	Noun	Complement	?

Don't forget to add the question marks. Spanish has the particularity to have two question marks: "¿" at the beginning, and "?" at the end of the question.

The intonation is also important in spoken Spanish. Since you cannot see the question marks when you're talking with people, you will have to hear how they give the right intonation when asking. It's not too different from English; just raise your voice a little at the end of the question.

If you want to ask about specific information, you can use the following words:

1. ¿Qué?
2. ¿Cuándo?
3. ¿Dónde?
4. ¿Por qué?
5. ¿Cuál?
6. ¿Cuáles?

1. What?
2. When?

3. Where?
4. Why?
5. Which one?
6. Which ones?

These information questions are placed before the verb and the noun, so they will always appear at the beginning of the question. The structure of these questions would be like this:

¿	Qué/Cuándo/Cómo/ Dónde/Por qué/Cuál	Verbo	Sujeto	Complement	?
	What/when/how/wher why/which one	verb	Noun	Complement	?

Let's see some examples of questions in Spanish:

¿Qué dijo el profesor sobre nuestro proyecto?
What did the teacher say about our project?

¿Dónde está la casa de María?
Where's María's house?

¿Por qué te fuiste temprano de la fiesta?
Why did you get out of the party early?

¿A dónde te vas?
Where are you going?

The past tense gives you an opportunity to use the comparative form of adjectives. Now you will learn how you can compare past circumstances to present ones with the comparative and superlative form of verbs in Spanish:

El comparativo

The comparative form, as its name reveals, it's what we use to compare adjectives and even adverbs in Spanish. The comparative form in Spanish is divided into three:

El comparativo de inferioridad – The comparative of inferiority

The comparative of inferiority is used to indicate one quality is inferior to another. To form the comparative of inferiority, you need to follow this structure:

sustantivo	verbo	menos	adjetivo	que	sustantivo
noun	verb	less	adjective	than	noun

Let's see some examples:

Jorge es menos alto que Rodrigo
Jorge is less tall than Rodrigo

300

| Ryan corre menos rápido que Cole |
| Ryan runs less fast than Cole |

| Fabián es menos gordo que Jorge |
| Fabián is less fat than Jorge |

If you want to form the negative form of these sentences, you can place **no** before the main verb:

| Jorge no es menos alto que Rodrigo |
| Jorge is not less tall than Rodrigo |

| Fabián no es menos gordo que Jorge |
| Fabián is not less fat than Jorge |

You can also compare objects:

sustantivo	verbo	menos	sustantivo	que	sustantivo
noun	verb	less	noun	than	noun

Some examples of this are:

| Yo tengo menos dinero que mi padre |
| I have less money than my father |

| Ellas comen menos comida que yo |
| They eat less food than me |

Nosotros tenemos menos mascotas que ustedes
We have less food than you

You can place **no** before the main verb to form the negative form of these sentences:

Yo no tengo menos dinero que mi padre
I don't have less money than my father

Ellas no comen menos comida que yo
They don't eat less food than me

- *El comparativo de superioridad – The comparative of superiority*

The comparative of superiority is used to indicate that one quality is superior to another. Its structure is as follows:

sustantivo	verbo	más	adjetivo/adverbio	que	sustantivo
noun	verb	more	adjective/adverb	than	noun

Let's see some examples:

Juan es más guapo que Raúl
Juan is more handsome than Raul.

Diego habla más rápido que José
Diego speaks faster than José.

| María corre más rápido que Ariana |
| Maria runs faster than Ariana |

If you want to form the negative form of these sentences, you just need to place **no** before the verb:

| Juan no es más guapo que Raúl |
| Juan is not more handsome than Raul. |

| Diego no habla más rápido que José |
| Diego doesn't speak faster than José does. |

Just like the comparative of inferiority, you can compare other nouns, too:

sustantivo	verbo	más	sustantivo	que	sustantivo
noun	verb	more	noun	than	noun

Let's see some examples:

| Ellos tienen más libros que yo |
| They have more books than I do |

| María y Juan tienen más dinero que mi mamá y mi papá |
| María and Juan have more money than my mom and my dad |

Mis amigos tienen más ropa que yo
My friends have more clothes than me

The negative form of these sentences are:

Ellos no tienen más libros que yo
They don't have more books than me

María no tiene más dinero que mi mamá
María doesn't more money than my mom.

- *El comparativo de igualdad – The comparative of equality*

The comparative of equality is used to indicate that qualities and nouns are equal to others. The structure of the comparative of equality is as follows:

sustantivo	verbo	tan	adjetivo/adverb	como	sustantivo
noun	verb	as	adjective/adverb	as	noun

Let's see some examples:

Yo era tan alto como José cuando yo era joven
I used to be as tall as José when I was young

Nosotros corremos tan rápido como ustedes
We run as fast as you do

If you want to compare nouns, then you'll have to use **tanto** rather than **tan:**

sustantivo	verbo	tanto	noun	como	sustantivo
noun	verb	as	noun	as	noun

Some examples are:

Ellos tienen tanto dinero como mis padres
They have as much money as my parents

Nosotros comemos tanta comida como ustedes
We eat as much food as you

Just like with the other comparatives, you can form the negative form of these sentences if you place **no** before the main verb:

Yo no era tan alto como José cuando yo era joven
I didn't use to be as tall as José when I was young

Nosotros no corremos tan rápido como ustedes
We don't as fast as you do

Ellos no tienen tanto dinero como mis padres
They don't have as much money as my parents

Nosotros no comemos tanta comida como ustedes
We don't eat as much food as you

As you may have also noticed, when using the comparative nouns with the comparative of equality, the word **tanto** has to correspond to the gender and number of the noun that's being used in the comparison.

El superlative – The superlative

The superlative is used to indicate that one quality or noun is the greatest of all. In Spanish, there are two types of superlatives:

- *El superlativo relativo – The relative superlative*

The structure of the relative superlative is:

sustantivo	verbo	artículo	más/menos	adjetivo	de	complemento
noun	verb	article	more/less	adjective	of/in	complement

Let's see some examples:

Yo soy el más alto del salón
I'm tallest in the classroom

Ellos son los más fuertes de la ciudad.
They're the strongest in the city

Ellos son los más graciosos de todos

They're the funniest of all
Ese libro es el más grande la librería
That book is the biggest in the bookshop

Ella es la profesora más inteligente de todas
She's the most intelligent teacher of all

- *El superlative absolute – The absolute relative*

The structure of the absolute relative is:

Sustantivo	Verbo	Adjetivo con la terminación *–ísimo*
Noun	Verb	Adjective with the termination *-ísimo*

Let's see some examples:

Estoy tristísimo
I'm very sad

Esta ropa es hermosísima
These clothes are the most beautiful

Esa computadora es carísima
That computer is very expensive. / That computer is the most expensive

Exercises:

I. Fill in the blanks with the right conjugation of the verb *ser:*

1. Yo no _ el profesor.

2. Ellos _ mis mejores amigos.

3. Mi mejor amiga _ francesa.

4. Ella viene de Perú. Ella es _ .

5. Veo que Juan _ muy inteligente.

6. La computadora _ mía.

II. Write the conjugation of the verb **estar**:

1. Yo no _ enfermo.

2. El papá de Juan _ en el hospital.

3. Mi mamá y yo _ en el supermercado.

4. Mis amigos _ afuera de mi casa.

5. La pelota _ muy sucia. Necesitamos levarla

III. Write the right form of the reflexive verb that's shown in parenthesis:

1. Yo _ (acostarse) a las 8 de la noche.

2. Ellos _ (vestirse) muy bien.

3. Mi hermana _ (maquillarse) mucho.

4. Yo _ (encontrarse) muy mareado

5. Ella _ (ponerse) la ropa que su mamá le compró.

IV. Write the preterite form of these verbs:

1. Ella come mucho –

2. Yo uso mi celular –

3. Ella quiere ir a la fiesta –

4. Ella escucha las noticias –

5. Ella está en mi casa –

V. Write the imperfect form of the following sentences:

1. Rodrigo come un helado –

2. Ella trabaja como mesera –

3. Nosotros preguntamos al profesor –

4. Mi amiga y yo somos muy altas –

5. Mis padres ven al perro crecer –

VI. Turn these sentences into questions:

1. María juega todas las tardes

2. Fabián está leyendo un libro de historia

3. Rodrigo mira televisión todos los días

4. Juan quiere salir conmigo

5. Mariana tiene mucho dinero

VII. Try to find the missing words that are needed to complete the comparative of inferiority:

1. Jorge es _ alto _ Fabián

2. David es _ inteligente _ Jorge.

3. Yo soy _ gordo _ mi hermano menor.

4. Mi hermano menor es _ rápido _ que yo.

5. Yo tengo _ dinero _ mi papá

6. Ella comió _ comida _ yo.

7. Mi mejor amigo tiene _ mascotas _ yo.

VIII. Find the right words and complete the comparative of superiority:

1. Diego habla _ rápido _ Jorge.

2. Tomás es _ alto _ Fabián

3. Jorge tiene _ dinero _ yo.

4. Mariana canta _ bonito _ que Julia

5. Alberto es _ alto _ Javier

6. Ella ha practicado por _ tiempo _ Fabiana

IX. Write the superlative form of the verbs in parenthesis. You can use the relative and absolute superlatives:

1. Jorge es _ (alto) de toda la clase

2. Nicolás es el perro_ (grande) que he visto en mi vida.

3. Ella es _ (hermosa)

4. La he llamado. Ella debe estar _ (ocupada)

5. Ella está _ (contenta) porque ha ganado un premio.

6. Mi mejor amigo es la persona _ (fuerte) que conozco.

7. Ellos son _ (fuerte)

Now that you have learned how Spanish is structured, you're ready to learn the vocabulary that will help you communicate effectively. In the following chapter, you'll find the most common phrases that will come very in handy if you're thinking about traveling abroad or talking with a native speaker.

Chapter 3: Useful Dialogue for Beginners

Meeting and Greetings:

In Spanish, there are many ways to greet someone and also to introduce yourself:

Spanish
1. ¡Buenos días!
2. Hola
3. ¡Buenas noches!
4. ¡Buenas tardes!

English
1. Good morning!
2. Hi!/Hello

3. Good evening! /Good night!
4. Good afternoon!

If you want to ask how a person is:

1. ¿Cómo estás?
2. ¿Cómo andas?
3. ¿Cómo te va?
4. ¿Cómo te encuentras?

1. How are you?
2. How are you doing?
3. How's it going?
4. How are you?

And also:

1. ¿Cómo **está**?
2. ¿Cómo **anda**?
3. ¿Cómo **le** va?
4. ¿Cómo **se encuentra**?

1. How are you?
2. How are you doing?
3. How's it going?
4. How are you?

At first sight, it might seem that the charts shown above have the same content, but as indicated by the bold words, there are subtle differences. The first chart is used when you're talking with a close friend or acquaintance, a relative, or someone your age.

The second chart is used in more polite settings: talking to a teacher, someone in a position of authority, a police officer, someone who you meet for the first time, someone older than you and so on.

How can you answer these questions? Take a look at the possible answers:

1.	Estoy bien.
2.	Me va bien.
3.	Estoy muy bien, gracias.
4.	Me encuentro bien, gracias.

1.	I'm fine.
2.	It's going well
3.	I'm fine, thank you.
4.	I'm fine, thank you.

If you want to introduce yourself:

Me llamo...	My name is...
Tengo 18 años	I'm 18 years old
Vengo de...	I come from
Mi nombre es...	My name is
Trabajo de...	I work as a...

And if you want to ask someone:

1. ¿Cómo te llamas?
2. ¿De dónde vienes?
3. ¿A que te dedicas?
4. ¿Cuál es tu nombre?
5. ¿Cuántos años tienes?

1. What's your name?
2. Where do you come from?

3. What do you do for a living?
4. What's your name?
5. How old are you?

Again, these questions also have a polite form:

1. ¿Cómo **se llama**?
2. ¿Cuál es **su** nombre?
3. ¿De dónde **viene**?
4. ¿A que **se dedica**?
5. ¿Cuántos años **tiene**?

1. What's your name?
2. What's your name?
3. Where do you come from?
4. What do you do for a living?
5. How old are you?

What if you want to say goodbye in Spanish? That's easy, just learn these phrases:

1. Adiós
2. ¡Nos vemos!
3. ¡Hasta pronto!
4. ¡Hasta luego!
5. ¡Hasta mañana!
6. ¡Nos vemos luego!

7. ¡Nos vemos pronto!
8. ¡Nos vemos mañana!
9. ¡Cuídate!
10. ¡Fue un gusto!   ¡Fue un placer!
11. ¡Fue un gusto haber conversado con usted!   ¡Fue un placer haber conversado con usted!
12. ¡Fue un gusto haberlo conocido!   ¡Fue un gusto haberlo conocido!
13. ¡Espero volverte a ver!   ¡Espero volver a verlo!

1. Goodbye
2. See you!
3. See you soon!
4. See you soon!
5. See you tomorrow!
6. See you soon!
7. See you soon!
8. See you tomorrow!
9. Take care of yourself!
10. It was a pleasure!
11. It was a pleasure to talk to you!

| 12. It was a pleasure to meet you! |
| 13. I hope to see you again! |

Let's see some conversations where these phrases are used:

- ¡Hola!
- ¡Hola!
- ¿Cómo te llamas?
- Me llamo Roberto. ¿Cómo te llamas tú?
- Yo me llamo Iván.
- Es un gusto conocerte, Iván.
- Gracias. También es un gusto conocerte.
- ¿A qué te dedicas?
- Yo soy profesor. ¿Y tú? ¿A qué te dedicas?
- Yo soy un ingeniero.
- ¿Cuántos años tienes, Roberto?
- Yo tengo 28 años, ¿y tú?
- Yo tengo 26.

This is the translation of the conversation:

- Hi!
- Hi!
- What's your name?
- My name is Roberto. What's your name?
- My name is Iván.

- It's a pleasure to meet you, Iván.
- Thank you. It's also a pleasure to meet you.
- What do you do for a living?
- I'm a teacher. And you? What do you do for a living?
- I'm an engineer
- How old are you, Roberto?
- I'm 28 years old, and you?
- I'm 26

Now let's see a more formal conversation:

- ¡Buenas tardes!
- ¡Buenas tardes! ¿Cómo se llama?
- Me llamo Juan. ¿Cómo se llama, usted?
- Me llamo Francisco. ¿Cómo se encuentra?
- Me encuentro muy bien, gracias. ¿Y usted? ¿Cómo se encuentra?
- Me encuentro muy bien. Gracias por preguntar. ¿De dónde viene?
- Yo vengo de México. ¿De dónde viene, usted?
- Yo vengo de Uruguay. ¿A qué se dedica?
- Pues, yo soy cantante.
- Ya veo.

And this is the translation of the story:

- ¡Good afternoon!
- ¡Good afternoon! What's your name?
- My name is Juan. What's your name?
- My name is Francisco. How are you?
- I'm very fine, thank you. And you? How are you?
- I'm very fine. Thanks for asking. Where do you come from?
- I come from Mexico. Where do you come from?
- I come from Uruguay. What do you do for a living?
- Well, I'm a singer.
- I see

Finally, let's see one final conversation. This is a conversation between two close friends:

- ¡Hola, Juan!
- ¡Hola, Fabián! ¿Cómo estás?

- Estoy bien. ¿Qué hay de ti?

- Pues, también estoy bien, gracias.

- Sabes, no me acuerdo cuántos años tienes, Juan.

- Yo tengo 18 años. ¿Cuántos años tienes tú, Fabián?

- Yo tengo 19. ¿Estás trabajando?

- Sí, estoy trabajando con mi papá.

- ¿A qué te dedicas?

- Soy panadero. ¿Y tú? ¿Estás trabajando?

- No. No estoy trabajando.

- ¿Estás estudiando?

- Sí. Estoy estudiando en la universidad.

- Pues, ¡qué bien! ¿Sabes qué hora es?

- Sí, son las 3 en punto.

- ¡O, no!

- ¿Pasa algo?

- ¡Tengo que ir a trabajar!

- Entiendo. ¡Corre! Espero que no llegues tarde.

- ¡Nos vemos luego!

- ¡Nos vemos!

And this is the translation of the conversation:

- Hi, Juan!

- Hi, Fabián! How are you?

- I'm fine. What about you?

- Well, I'm also fine, thank you.
- You know, I can't remember how old you are, Juan.
- I'm 18 years old. How old are you, Fabián?
- I'm 19. Are you working?
- Yes, I'm working with my dad.
- What are you doing?
- I'm a baker. And you? Are you working?
- No, I'm not working.
- Are you studying?
- Yes. I'm studying in college.
- Well, ithat's great! Do you know what time is?
- Yes, it's 3 o'clock
- Oh, no!
- What's wrong?
- I have to go to work!
- I understand. Run! I hope you don't arrive late!
- See you later!

See you!

If you want to answer about your job, you can say:

Soy / Trabajo como:	I am / I work as:
• Un profesor/ una profesora	• A teacher
	• An engineer
	• A writer

• Un ingeniero/ una ingeniera	• A doctor
• Un escritor/ una escritora	• A baker
• Un doctor/ una doctora	• A fireman/ firewoman
• Un panadero/ una panadera	• An actor/ an actress
• Un bombero/una bombera	• An electrician
• Un actor/ una actriz	
• Un/ una electricista	

Now that you know how to greet and introduce yourself. Let's keep moving and learn more vocabulary.

At the Restaurant

If you go to a restaurant, what should you have in mind? Many things, of course. The first thing that might come up in your mind is the place. Try these Spanish phrases to decide and ask for other's opinions on the restaurant you want to go:

1. ¿A dónde vamos?
2. ¿A dónde quieres ir?
3. ¿A dónde **quieren** ir?
4. ¿Qué quieres comer?
5. ¿Ya has ido a este restaurante anteriormente?
6. ¿Ya **han** ido a este restaurante anteriormente? (Plural)
7. ¿Qué restaurantes conoces?
8. ¿Conoces algún restaurante cerca de aquí?
9. ¿Conoces algún restaurante de comida china?

10. ¿Qué se te antoja?
11. Quiero ir a un restaurante de comida italiana
12. No quiero comer en un restaurante de lujo
13. Quiero ir a un restaurante barato
14. Conozco un restaurante que te encantará
15. ¿Quiénes irán al restaurante?

And this is the translation of the phrases:

1. Where do we go?
2. Where do you want to go?
3. Where do you want to go?
4. What do you want to eat?
5. Have you been to this restaurant before?
6. Have you been to this restaurant before?
7. What restaurants do you know?
8. Do you know any restaurant near here?
9. Do you know any Chinese food restaurant?
10. What do you crave? /What would you like to eat?
11. I want to go to an Italian food restaurant.
12. I don't want to eat in a fancy restaurant
13. I want to go to a cheap restaurant
14. I know a restaurant that you will love
15. Who will go to the restaurant?

After you have decided what restaurant you to go, you need to know how to order and ask for some unknown dishes. Take a look at the following phrases:

1. ¿Ya llegamos al restaurante?
2. ¿Qué piensas ordenar?
3. Ordenaré lo más barato.
4. ¿Dónde está el menu?
5. No sé leer el menú
6. ¿Cuánto cuesta este platillo?
7. ¿Ya has probado este platillo?
8. ¿Por qué no pides este platillo?
9. ¿Es delicioso este platillo?
10. ¿Dónde están las bebidas?
11. ¿Dónde está el baño?
12. ¿Eres alérgico a algo?
13. ¿Te gusta el pescado?
14. No me gusta el pescado
15. ¿Hay postres?
16. ¿Venden tacos?
17. ¿Dónde está el mesero?

1. Have we arrived at the restaurant?
2. What do you want to order?
3. I'll order the cheapest dish.

4. Where's the menu?
5. I don't know how to read the menu.
6. How much is this dish?
7. Have you eaten this dish before?
8. Why don't you order this dish?
9. Is this dish delicious?
10. Where are the drinks?
11. Where's the bathroom?
12. Are you allergic to anything?
13. Do you like fish?
14. I don't like fish
15. Are there desserts?
16. Do they sell tacos?
17. Where's the waiter?

While eating, a conversation might take place, or maybe you just want to tell everyone you're enjoying your dish. Whatever it is you want to do, these following phrases will surely help you:

1. ¡La comida está deliciosa!
2. ¡Este platillo está delicioso!
3. ¡Me encanta este platillo!
4. ¡Debes probar este platillo!
5. ¡Mis felicitaciones al chef!

6. ¿Qué piensas de tu platillo?
7. ¿Te gusta tu platillo?
8. ¿Te gusta lo que estás comiendo?
9. ¡Me encanta!
10. ¡No me gusta!
11. ¡Está horrible!
12. No lo recomiendo
13. Puede estar mejor
14. Necesita más sal
15. No me gusta para nada
16. ¿Puedo pedir más?
17. ¿Puedo pedir otro platillo?

1. The food is delicious!
2. This dish is delicious!
3. I love this dish!
4. You must try this dish!
5. My compliments to the chef!
6. What do you think about your dish?
7. Do you like your dish?
8. Do you like what you're eating?
9. I love it!
10. I don't like it!
11. It's horrible!

12. I don't recommend it	
13. It can be better	
14. It needs more salt	
15. I don't like it all.	
16. Can I ask for more?	
17. Can I ask for another dish?	

Ok, you have enjoyed your meal. That's great. But you now that someone might have to pay for all you have eaten. Learn these phrases so that the situation doesn't catch you unprepared:

¿Cuánto cuesta este platillo?	How much is this dish?
¿Quién pagará por este platillo?	Who will pay for this dish?
¿Pagaremos todos?	Will we all pay?
¿Dividiremos la cuenta?	Will we split the bill?
¿Puedo pagar yo?	Can I pay?
Quiero pagar por ti	I want to pay for you
Yo lo pagaré	I'll pay for it
No tengo dinero	I don't have money
Yo invitaré	It's on me
¿Aceptan tarjetas de crédito?	Do they accept credit cards?

¿Aceptan dinero en efectivo?	Do they accept cash?
¿Aceptan tarjetas de débito?	Do they accept debit cards?
¿Deberíamos dar propina?	Should we tip?
Cada uno pagará por su platillo	Each one will have to pay for his meal

After paying, you can thank your hosts by saying:

Gracias por invitarme a cenar con ustedes	Thanks for inviting me to have dinner with you
De nada	You're welcome
Disfruté mucho su compañía	I enjoyed your company a lot
Me gusto mucho haber cenado con ustedes	I liked very much to have dinner with you
Gracias por venir	Thanks for coming
Debemos salir nuevamente	We should go out again
¿Cuándo volvemos a salir?	When will we go out again?

Let's see some conversations:

• ¿A dónde iremos a cenar esta noche?	• Where will we go to eat out tonight?

330

• No lo sé. ¿A dónde quisieras ir a comer?	• I don't know. Where would you like to go to eat out?
• ¿Conoces algún restaurante cerca de aquí?	• Do you know any restaurant near here?
• Sí. Conozco un restaurante de comida italiana cerca de aquí.	• Yes. I know an Italian food restaurant near here.
• ¿Has ido a ese restaurante anteriormente?	• Have you been to that restaurant before?
• Sí, he ido a ese restaurante muchas veces con mis amigos.	• Yes, I've been to that restaurant many times with my friends
• Entonces, está decidido. ¡Vamos!	• Then, it's decided!

• ¿A qué restaurante iremos?	• What restaurant will we go to?
• Iremos a un restaurante de comida china.	• We will go to a Chinese food restaurant.
• No me gusta la comida china. ¿Conoces algún otro restaurant?	• I don't like Chinese food. Do you know any other restaurant?

• Sí. Conozco un restaurante de comida tailandesa. ¿Quisieras ir a ese restaurante?	• Yes. I know a Thai food restaurant. Would you like to go to that restaurant?
• ¿Es un restuarante de lujo?	• Is it a fancy restaurant?
• Sí. La comida en ese restaurante es muy cara.	• Yes. Food there is very expensive
• No tengo mucho dinero.	• I don't have much money.
• Entiendo.	• I understand
• ¿Por qué no vamos a otro restaurante? Yo conozco otro restaurant de comida china cerca de aquí. Y lo mejor de todo es que la comida allí es muy barata.	• Why don't we go to another restaurant? I know another Chinese food restaurant near here. And the best of all is that the food there is very cheap.
• Suena como una buena idea. ¡Vamos!	

• ¿Qué piensas de tu platillo? ¿Te gusta?	• What do you think of your dish? Do you like it?
• Sí. ¡Me encanta!	• Yes. I love it!
• Sabía que te iba a gustar. Tu mama me dijo que a ti	

te gustaba la comida china.

- ¿Qué hay de ti? ¿Te gustó tu platillo?

- Bueno, estuvo delicioso, pero no me gustó mucho.

- ¿Por qué no?

- Porque creo que le faltó un poco de sal.

- Bueno, no te preocupes mucho.

- Creo que tenemos que pagar ya.

- Sí. ¿Cuánto cuesta este platillo?

- Tu platillo cuesta 15 dólares y el mío cuesta 20 dólares.

- ¿Dividimos la cuenta?

- No. Creo que sería mejor si tú pagas por lo que comiste y yo pago por mi platillo.

- I knew that you would like it. Your mom told me that you liked Chinese food.

- What about you? Did you like your dish?

- Well, it was delicious, but I didn't like it very much.

- Why not?

- Because I think that it needed more salt.

- Well, don't worry too much.

- I think we have to pay now

- Yes. How much is this dish?

- Your dish is 15 dollars and mine is 20 dollars.

- Should we split the bill?

- No. I think it would be better if you pay for what you ate and I pay for my dish.

• Suena bien. ¿Sabes si aceptan tarjetas de crédito?	• That sounds good. Do you know if they accept credit cards?
• No lo sé.	• I don't know.
• ¿Cómo vas a pagar tú?	• How are you going to pay?
• Voy a pagar en efectivo.	
• Será mejor que pregunte al mesero si aceptan mi tarjeta.	• I'm going to pay in cash.
	• I'd better ask the waiter if they accept my card.
• Es una buena idea.	• It's a good idea.
• Gracias por invitarme a cenar.	• Thanks for inviting me to have dinner
• Gracias por venir.	• Thanks for coming.

At the Hotel:

When you want to stay at a hotel, you need to ask for as much information as you need. What questions will help you find the best deals?

Spanish
1. ¿Cómo se llama este hotel?
2. ¿Qué tipo de hotel estás buscando?
3. ¿Buscas un hotel de lujo?
4. ¿Qué comodidades estás buscando?
5. ¿Dónde quieres hospedarte?
6. ¿Quieres que el hotel tenga una piscina?
7. ¿Tiene este hotel una piscina?
8. ¿Tiene este hotel un gimnasio?
9. ¿Cuánto cuesta la habitación?
10. Quiero una habitación matrimonial.
11. Quiero una habitación de lujo
12. ¿Está este hotel cerca del aeropuerto?
13. ¿Está este hotel en el centro de la ciudad?
14. ¿Está este hotel cerca del paradero de bus?

And this is the translation of the phrases:

English
1. What's the name of this hotel?
2. What type of hotel are you looking for?
3. Are you looking for a fancy hotel?
4. What amenities are you looking for?
5. Where do you want to stay?
6. Do you want the hotel to have a pool?
7. Does this hotel have a pool?

8. Does this hotel have a gym?
9. How much does the room cost?
10. I want a double room
11. I want a luxury room.
12. Is this hotel near the airport?
13. Is this hotel in the city center?
14. Is this hotel near the bus stop?

Once you have found the hotel you want to stay at, you need to make yourself feel like home. Use these phrases so you can have a great time at the hotel:

1. ¿Cuál es el número de mi habitación?
2. Mi número de habitación es 302
3. ¿En qué piso está mi habitación?
4. Mi habitación está en el tercer piso
5. Mi habitación está sucia
6. Tienes que mostrar tu identificación
7. ¿Tengo que dejar propina?
8. ¿Dónde está piscina?
9. ¿Dónde está el gimnasio?
10. ¿Dónde están las toallas?
11. ¿Tengo que pagar para entrar al gimnasio?
12. ¿A quién debo llamar si hay una emergencia?
13. ¿Cuál es el número del servicio a la habitación?
14. ¿Cuál es el número de la recepción?

15. ¿Quién llevará mis maletas?
16. ¿Dónde está el comedor?
17. ¿Dónde está la oficina?
18. ¿Dónde está el restaurante?
19. ¿Pueden traer el desayuno a mi habitación?
20.¿Pueden llamarme para despertarme, por favor?

And this is the translation of the phrases:

1. What's my room number?
2. My room number is 302
3. What floor is my room on?
4. My room is on the third floor.
5. My room is dirty.
6. You have to show your ID
7. Do I have to leave a tip?
8. Where's the pool?
9. Where's the gym?
10. Where are the towels?
11. Do I have to pay to enter the gym?
12. Who should I call if there's an emergency?
13. What's the number of room service?
14. What's the number of the reception?
15. Who will carry my bags?
16. Where's the lunchroom?
17. Where's the office?

18. Where's the restaurant?
19. Can you bring breakfast to my room?
20. Can you give me a wake-up call?

Let's see some conversations where these phrases are used:

• ¿Qué estás haciendo?	• What are you doing?
• Estoy buscando un hotel.	• I am looking for a hotel.
• ¿Qué tipo de hotel estás buscando?	• What type of hotel are you looking for?
• Estoy buscando un hotel que está cerca del aeropuerto.	• I am looking for a hotel that is near the airport.
• ¿Estás buscando un hotel de lujo?	• Are you looking for a luxury hotel?
• No. No quiero gastar mucho dinero.	• No. I don't want to spend a lot of money.
• Conozco un hotel que te va a gustar. Es un hotel que está cerca del aeropuerto y no está muy caro.	• I know a hotel that you will like. It is a hotel that is close to the airport and not very expensive.
• ¿En serio? ¿Cómo se llama el hotel?	• Seriously? What is the name of the hotel?
• El hotel se llama "Costa Grande"	• The hotel is called "Costa Grande"

338

• ¿Qué comodidades tiene ese hotel?	• What amenities does this hotel have?
• Tiene una piscina, un spa, un gimnasio, un restaurante y más.	• It has a pool, a spa, a gym, a restaurant and more.
• ¡Vaya! Espero que no sea muy caro!	• Wow! I hope it is not very expensive!
• No te preocupes. Yo me que´de en ese hotel el año pasado y no fue para nada caro.	• Don't worry. I stayed at that hotel last year and it was not expensive at all.

• ¡Buenas tardes! Reservé un habitación en este hotel hace una semana.	• Good afternoon! I booked a room at this hotel a week ago.
• ¿Cómo se llama?	• What is your name?
• Me llamo Francisco Armín.	• My name is Francisco Armín.
• ¿Podría mostrarme su identificación?	• Could you show me your ID?
• ¡Claro! Aquí está.	• Sure! Here it is.
• Ya confirmé que usted es verdaderamente Francisco Armín.	• I've confirmed that you truly are Francisco Armín.

• ¡Genial! ¿Dónde está mi habitación? ¿Cuál es el número de mi habitación?	• Great! Where is my room? What is my room number?
• Su habitación está en el quinto piso. El número de su habitación es 510.	• Your room is on the fifth floor. Your room number is 510.
• Gracias. ¿Dónde está el elevador?	• Thank you. Where is the elevator?
• El elevador está cerca de las escaleras.	• The elevator is near the stairs.
• ¿Quién llevará mis maletas?	• Who will carry my bags?
• El botones llevará sus maletas.	• The bellhop will carry your bags.
• Gracias.	• Thank you.

At the Gas Station

What should you say when you're at a gas station? Take a look at the following phrases and see if you can use them:

1. ¿Dónde está la gasolinera?
2. ¿Dónde está gasolinera más cercana?
3. ¿Cuánto cuesta la gasolina?
4. ¿Está cara la gasolina aquí?
5. ¿Puedes mostrarme dónde está la gasolinera?

1. Where's the gas station?
2. Where's the nearest gas station?
3. How much does gasoline cost?
4. Is gasoline expensive here?
5. Can you show me where the gas station is?

Let's see some conversations where these phrases are used:

- ¡Buenas tardes!

- ¡Buenas tardes! ¿En qué le puedo ayudar?

- Quisiera poner gasolina en mi auto.

- ¿Cuánta gasolina desea?

- Quisiera 10 litros de gasolina.

- ¿Qué tipo de gasolina quisiera?

- Quisiera la de 95, por favor.

- El galón de gasolina de 95 cuesta $5 por litro. ¿Está bien?

- Sí. Me parece bien.

- ¿Cómo desea pagar?

- Quisiera pagar con tarjeta de crédito

- Hay un descuento de 5 dólares si usted compra 15 galones de gasolina.

- Me parece una muy buena oferta. Entonces, quisiera comprar 15 galones de gasolina.

- ¡Genial! Ya está

- Gracias.

- ¡Tenga un buen día!

- Good afternoon!

- Good afternoon! How can I help you?

- I would like to put gasoline in my car.

- How much gasoline do you want?
- I want 10 liters of gasoline.
- What type of gasoline would you like?
- I want 95, please.
- The gallon of 95 costs $ 5 per liter. Is it okay?
- Yes. It seems fine.
- How would you like to pay?
- I would like to pay by credit card
- There is a $ 5 discount if you buy 15 gallons of gasoline.
- I think it's a very good offer. So, I would like to buy 15 gallons of gasoline.
- Great! It's done
- Thank you.
- Have a nice day!

At the Mall

When you go shopping, you might find it very useful to remember the following phrases:

1. ¿Dónde está el centro comercial?
2. ¿Qué puedo encontrar en el centro comercial?
3. ¿Está el centro comercial abierto?
4. ¿Qué tiendas encontraré en este centro comercial?
5. ¿Hay una tienda de muebles en este centro comercial?
6. ¿Cuánto está este mueble?
7. ¿Dónde está tienda de electrónicos?
8. ¿Dónde puedo encontrar un cargador de celular?
9. Puedes encontrarlo en la tienda de electrónicos
10. ¿Aceptan tarjetas de crédito?

11. ¿Tienen alguna oferta disponible?
12. ¿Hay algún descuento?
13. Hay 10% de descuento en este producto.
14. Hay una oferta de dos por tres.
15. No tenemos descuentos disponibles
16. ¿Dónde está la tienda de ropa de hombres?
17. ¿Dónde está la tienda de ropa de mujeres?
18. ¿Cuánto cuesta este vestido?
19. Este vestido cuesta 30 dólares
20. ¿Cuánto cuesta esta blusa?
21. Está blusa cuesta 50 dólares
22. ¿Tiene este vestido en un tamaño más pequeño?
23. ¿Tiene este vestido en un tamaño más grande?
24. Este vestido es muy apretado
25. Este vestido es muy suelto
26. No me gusta este pantalón
27. ¿Dónde está la sección de ropa para bebés?
28. Esta es la sección de ropa para bebés
29. ¿Tiene más vestidos?
30. ¿Dónde está el estacionamiento?

1. Where's the shopping mall?
2. What can I find at the shopping mall?
3. Is the shopping mall open?

4. What stores will I find in this shopping mall?
5. Is there a furniture store in this mall?
6. How much is this piece of furniture?
7. Where is the electronics store?
8. Where can I find a phone charger?
9. You can find it in the electronics store.
10. Do you accept credit cards?
11. Do you have any available offer?
12. Is there any discount?
13. There is a 10% discount on this product.
14. There is a three-for-two offer
15. We don't have any available discounts.
16. Where is the men's clothing store?
17. Where is the women's clothing store?
18. How much does this dress cost?
19. This dress costs $30
20. How much does this blouse cost?
21. This blouse costs $50
22. Do you have this dress in a smaller size?
23. Do you have this dress in a larger size?
24. This dress is very tight
25. Este vestido es muy flojo
26. I don't like this dress
27. Where is the baby clothes section?

28. This is the baby clothes section.
29. Do you have more dresses?
30. Where's the parking lot?

Now let's take a look at some conversations where these phrases are used:

• Gracias por venir conmigo al centro comercial.	• Thank you for coming with me to the mall.
• ¿Es la primera vez que vienes a este centro comercial?	• Is it the first time you come to this mall?
• Sí. Nunca he venido antes a este centro comercial	• Yes. I have never come to this mall before
• ¿Qué piensas comprar?	• What do you want to buy?
• Quiero comprar un cargador de celular y también ropa para mí.	• I want to buy a cell phone charger and also clothes for me.
• Pues has venido al lugar indicado. En este centro comercial encontrarás todo lo que estás buscando.	• Well, you have come to the right place. In this mall, you will find everything you are looking for.
	• Do you know if there are offers available?

- ¿Sabes si hay ofertas disponibles?
- No lo sé. Pero puedes preguntar a los vendedores. Ellos te pueden ayudar.
- ¿Dónde está la tienda de electrónicos?
- La tienda de electrónicos está en el segundo piso.
- ¿Este centro comercial tiene segundo piso?
- Sí, si quieres ir a la tienda de electrónicos, tendrás que usar las escaleras eléctricas.
- ¿Y dónde está la tienda de ropa?
- La tienda de ropa está cerca a la tienda de electrónicos.
- Parece que conoces muy bien este centro comercial. ¿Vienes a este

- I don't know. But you can ask the sellers. They can help you.
- Where is the electronics store?
- The electronics store is on the second floor.
- Does this mall have a second floor?
- Yes, if you want to go to the electronics store, you will have to use the escalators.
- And where is the clothing store?
- The clothing store is close to the electronics store.
- You seem to know this mall very well. Do you come to this mall often?
- I come every weekend with my friends to watch a movie.

centro comercial a menudo?	• Is there also a cinema in this mall?
• Vengo todos los fines de semana con mis amigos a ver una película.	• Yes. Do you want me to show it to you?
• ¿También hay un cine en este centro comercial?	
• Sí. ¿Quieres que te lo muestre?	

Let's take a look at another conversation:

• ¡María! ¡Qué gusto verte aquí en este centro comercial!	• Mary! What a pleasure to see you here in this mall!
• ¡Hola, Ariana! También es un gusto verte. ¿Qué estás haciendo aquí?	• Hello Ariana! It is also nice to see you. What are you doing here?
• He venido a ete centro comercial porque quiero comprar un nuevo celular para mi hermano menor.	• I have come to this mall because I want to buy a new cell phone for my younger brother.
• ¿En serio? ¿Piensas regalarle un celular?	• Really? Do you plan to give him a cell phone?
	• That's right. I'm sure he will love the new cell

- Así es. Estoy seguro que le va a encantar el nuevo celular que he comprado para él.
- ¿Ya lo compraste? ¿Dónde está?
- Esta aquí en la bolsa.
- ¿Puedo verlo?
- ¡Claro!
- ¡Vaya! Es un celular muy bonito. ¿Dónde lo compraste?
- Lo compré en la tienda de celulares que está en el tercer piso.
- Ya veo. Creo que yo también compraré un nuevo celular.
- Veo que tienes muchas bolsas. ¿Qué has comprado?
- Compré ropa para mí y también para mi esposo.
- ¡Has comprado mucho!

- phone that I bought for him.
- You already bought it? Where is?
- It's here in the bag.
- Can I see it?
- Sure!
- Wow! It's a very pretty cell phone. Where did you buy it?
- I bought it at the cell phone store on the third floor.
- I see. I think I'll buy a new cell phone, too.
- I see you have many bags. What have you bought?
- I bought clothes for myself and also for my husband.
- You have bought a lot!
- There are many discounts available in the clothing store.

- Es que hay muchos descuentos disponibles en la tienda de ropa. Hay incluso una oferta de tres por dos en toda la ropa de hombres.
- ¿En serio? Creo que iré a la tienda de ropa también. Mi hijo también necesita ropa nueva.
- ¡Tienes que ir! Además, con toda la ropa que está en descuento, ahorrarás muchísimo dinero.
- Sí. Creo que tienes razón. Ahora mismo iré a la tienda.
- ¡Te veo luego!
- ¡Nos vemos!

- There is even a three-for-two offer on all men's clothing.
- Seriously? I think I'll go to the clothing store, too. My son also needs new clothes.
- You have to go! Also, with all the clothes that are on discount, you will save a lot of money.
- Yes. I think you are right. I will go to the store right now.
- See you later!
- See you!

At the Bank

Being abroad can already be very stressful. It's especially stressful if you have to deal with money issues in a different country. What can you say so that everyone around you understands what you're talking about?

Spanish
1. ¿Dónde está el banco?
2. ¿Dónde está el banco más cercano?
3. ¿Qué banco estás buscando?
4. Estoy buscando este banco
5. ¿Dónde está oficina central?
6. Quiero ir a la oficina central
7. Vengo para abrir una cuenta de ahorros
8. ¿En qué le podemos ayudar?
9. Quisiera abrir una cuenta de ahorros
10. Quisiera abrir una cuenta corriente
11. Quisiera hacer una transacción bancaria

12. Quisiera retirar dinero
13. Quisiera depositar dinero
14. ¿Dónde está el cajero automático más cercano?
15. ¿Debo esperar a que me llamen?
16. Quisiera tener una tarjeta de crédito
17. Quisiera tener una tarjeta de débito
18. Quisiera una cuenta de ahorros en dólares
19. Quisiera una cuenta de ahorros en euros
20. Yo soy el titular de la cuenta
21. Él es el titular de la cuenta
22. Tengo una chequera
23. ¿Dónde aceptan esta tarjeta?
24. ¿Cobran mantenimiento de cuenta?
25. ¿Hay cargos por retiro?
26. ¿Hay cargos por transferencia?
27. ¿Cuánto es la tasa de interés anual?
28. ¿Dónde puedo retirar dinero?
29. ¿Puedo hacer transferiencias en línea?
30. ¿Dónde está mi clave?
31. ¿Cuál es mi clave?
32. ¿Este es mi número de tarjeta?
33. ¿Quién puede ayudarme con mis preguntas?
34. ¿Cómo bloqueo la tarjeta?
35. ¿Cambian monedas extranjeras aquí?

36. ¿Dónde puedo pedir un préstamo?
37. ¿Qué documentos debo presentar?
38. Quiero un préstamo de 1500 dólares.

And this is the translation:

English
1. Where's the bank?
2. Where's the nearest bank?
3. What bank are you looking for?
4. I'm looking for this bank
5. Where's the head office?
6. I want to go to the head office.
7. I come to open a savings account
8. How can I help you?
9. I would like to open a savings account
10. I would like to open a checking account
11. I would like to make a bank transaction
12. I would like to withdraw money
13. I'd like to deposit some money
14. Where is the nearest ATM?
15. Should I wait to be called?
16. I would like to have a credit card
17. I would like to have a debit card
18. I would like a dollar savings account

19. I would like a savings account in euros
20. I am the account holder
21. He is the account holder
22. I have a checkbook
23. Where is this card accepted?
24. Do you charge account maintenance?
25. Are there any withdrawal fees?
26. Are there transfer fees?
27. How much is the annual interest rate?
28. Where can I withdraw money?
29. Can I make transfers online?
30. Where is my password?
31. What is my password?
32. Is this my card number?
33. Who can help me with my questions?
34. How do I lock the card?
35. Do you exchange foreign currencies here?
36. Where can I ask for a loan?
37. What documents should I submit?
38. I want a loan of 1500 dollars.

Now let's see some conversations where these phrases are used:

• ¡Buenas tardes!

- ¡Buenas tardes! ¿En qué podemos ayudarle?
- Quisiera abrir una cuenta de ahorros.
- Le puedo ayudar con eso, señor.
- Gracias.
- ¿Cuál es su nombre?
- Mi nombre es Juan.
- ¿Cuál es su apellido?
- Mi apellido es Ramirez.
- Muy bien. ¿Tiene algún document de identidad?
- Sí, tengo mi pasaporte.
- ¿Podría mostarmelo, por favor?
- ¡Claro! Aquí está.
- Gracias. Señor Razmirez, ¿cuántos años tiene?
- Tengo 35 años.
- ¿Dónde nació?
- Nací en Buenos Aires, Argentina.
- ¿Hace cuánto está usted en este país?
- He estado en este país por 5 años.
- Muy bien. ¿A qué se dedica?
- Soy profesor de matemáticas.
- ¿Dónde trabaja?
- Trabajo en una escuela secundaria en el centro de la ciudad.
- ¿Dónde vive?

- Yo vivo en Calle Almería 321.

- ¿Tiene esposa o hijos?

- Sí. Estoy casado y tengo 2 hijos.

- Muy bien. Por favor, firme estos documentos.

- Ya está. ¿Qué más debo hacer?

- Nada más. Ya todo lo necesario está hecho. Ahora lo que usted necesita hacer es esperar a que su tarjeta de débito llegue a su dirección.

- ¿Cuándo llegará mi tarjeta de débito?

- Llegará en 3 días.

- ¿Dónde aceptan esa tarjeta de débito?

- La aceptan en todas las tiendas que aceptan Visa.

- ¿Puedo retirar dinero con mi tarjeta de débito?

- ¡Claro que sí!

- ¿Qué debo hacer para retirar dinero de cuenta de ahorros?

- Usted puede usar su tarjeta de débito para retirar dinero de su cuenta. Lo que usted debe hacer es ir a un cajero automático e insertar su tarjeta de débito en el cajero automático. Luego, usted tendrá que indicar cuánto dinero quiere retirar.

- Suena bien. ¿Me cobran cargos adicionales por hacer retiros?

- No. Los retiros en los cajeros automáticos son totalmente gratuitos.
- ¿Cuánto dinero puedo retirar?
- Usted puede retirar un máximo de 3000 dólares por día.
- Entiendo.
- ¿Alguna otra pregunta, señor Ramirez?
- ¿Qué pasa si pierdo mi tarjeta?
- Usted puede llamar a este número que está aquí en este docuemento. Tiene que seguir las instrucciones que le digan para poder bloquear la tarjeta.
- ¿Puedo pedir otra tarjeta si la pierdo?
- Claro, y la nueva tarjeta es totalmente gratis también.

- Good afternoon!
- Good afternoon! How can we help you?
- I would like to open a savings account.
- I can help you with that, sir.
- Thank you.
- What's your name?
- My name is Juan.
- What is your last name?

- My last name is Ramirez.
- Ok. Do you have any identification documents?
- Yes, I have my passport.
- Could you show me, please?
- Sure! Here it is.
- Thank you. Mr. Razmirez, how old are you?
- I'm 35.
- Where were you born?
- I was born in Buenos Aires, Argentina.
- How long have you been in this country?
- I have been in this country for 5 years.
- OK. What do you do for a living?
- I am a math teacher.
- Where do you work?
- I work in a high school in the city center.
- Where do you live?
- I live in Calle Almería 321.
- Do you have a wife or children?
- Yes. I am married and have 2 children.
- OK. Please sign these documents.
- It's done. What else should I do?
- Nothing else. Everything necessary is already done. Now what you need to do is wait for your debit card to arrive at your address.

- When will my debit card arrive?
- It will arrive in 3 days.
- Where is that debit card accepted?
- They accept it in all stores that accept Visa.
- Can I withdraw money with my debit card?
- Of course!
- What should I do to withdraw money from a savings account?
- You can use your debit card to withdraw money from your account. What you should do is go to an ATM and insert your debit card into the ATM. Then, you will have to indicate how much money you want to withdraw.
- Sounds good. Am I charged additional fees for making withdrawals?
- No. Withdrawals at ATMs are completely free.
- How much money can I withdraw?
- You can withdraw a maximum of $ 3,000 per day.
- I get it.
- Any other questions, Mr. Ramirez?
- What happens if I lose my card?
- You can call this number that is here in this document. You have to follow the instructions they tell you to be able to lock the card.

Let's take a look at another conversation:

¡Buenas tardes!	Good afternoon!
¡Buenas tardes! ¿En qué podemos ayudarla?	Good afternoon! How can we help you?
Vengo a pedir un préstamo.	I've come to ask for a loan.
Yo le puedo ayudar con eso. ¿Cuál es su nombre?	I can help you with that. What's your name?
Mi nombre es María Ríos.	My name is María Ríos.
¿Tiene algún documento de identidad?	Do you have any identification documents?
Sí. ¿Quiere que se lo muestre?	Yes. Do you want me to show it to you?
Sí, por favor.	Yes, please.
Muy bien, señorita Ríos. Veo que usted ya es cliente nuestro.	Very well, Miss Rios. I see that you are already our client.
Así es. Yo tengo una tarjeta de crédito. La uso todos los días.	That's right. I have a credit card. I use it every day.

¡Qué bien! ¿Podría decirme cuanto dinero gastas todos los meses?	That's perfect! Could you tell me how much money you spend every month?
Gasto aproximadamente 600 dólares.	I spend approximately $ 600.
Entendido. ¿Cuánto dinero quisiera pedir?	Understood. How much money would you like to ask for?
Quisiera un préstamo de 6500 dólares.	I would like a loan of $ 6,500.
OK. Muy bien. Si usted desea pedir un préstamo de 6500 dólares, entonces tendrá que llenar este documento.	OK. Very well. If you wish to request a loan of $ 6,500, then you will have to fill out this document.
Lo haré.	I will.
¿Terminó?	Finished?
Sí, ya terminé. ¿Qué más debo hacer?	Yes, I've already finished. What else should I do?
¿Desea recibir el dinero en un cheque?	Do you want to receive the money in a check?
No. ¿Puedo recibir el dinero en mi cuenta de ahorros?	No. Can I receive the money in my savings account?
¿Tiene usted también una cuenta de ahorros?	Do you also have a savings account?

Sí. Yo soy el titular de una cuenta de ahorros.	Yes. I am the account holder of a savings account.
Muy bien. Deme un momento para poder ingresar la información.	Very well. Give me a moment to enter the information.
¿Desea que le de mi número de cuenta?	Do you want me to give you my account number?
No es necesario. Aquí tengo toda la información necesaria.	It's not necessary. Here I have all the necessary information.
¿Ya está hecho?	It's done?
Sí. Ya transferí el dinero a su cuenta de ahorros.	Yes. I already transferred the money to your savings account.
¡Genial! ¡Muchas gracias!	Great! Thank you very much!
No se preocupe. Estamos para ayudarla.	Don't worry. We are here to help you.

At the Hospital

In a perfect world, we wouldn't need to go to the doctor. Unfortunately, this is not a perfect world. While we hope you never get into trouble while you're abroad, it's still important for you to learn some Spanish phrases that might come very in handy in your new country:

Spanish	English
El cuidado médico en este hospital es muy bueno.	Medical care in this hospital is very good
¿Dónde está el hospital más cercano?	Where's the nearest hospital?
¿Dónde está la oficina del doctor?	Where's the doctor office?
¿Cuánto cuesta la cita médica en este hospital?	How much does the medical appointment in this hospital cost?

¿Tiene seguro médico?	Do you have medical insurance?
Yo tengo seguro médico	I have medical insurance
Yo no tengo seguro médico	I don't have medical insurance
¿Cómo puedo conseguir seguro médico?	How can I get medical insurance?
Mi seguro médico ha expirado	My medical insurance has expired.
¿Dónde te duele?	Where does it hurt?
¿Te duele aquí?	Does it hurt here?
Tienes que tomar estos medicamentos	You have to take these medications
Tienes que tomar estas pastillas	You have to take these pills
¿Cuánto cuestán estas pastillas?	How much do these pills cost?
¿Qué cubre mi seguro?	What does my insurance cover?
¿Dónde tengo que pagar?	Where do I have to pay?
¿Dónde puedo conseguir estas pastillas?	Where can I get these pills?
¿Dónde puedo conseguir estos medicamentos?	Where can I get these medications?
¿Necesito cirugía?	Do I need surgery?

Necesitas cirugía	You need surgery
¿Es una emergencia?	Is it an emergency?
Me duele mucho el estómago	My stomach hurts a lot
Me duelen mucho las piernas	My legs hurt a lot
Me duele mucho aquí	It hurts a lot here
¿Has comido algo?	Have you eaten anything?
¿Eres alérgico a algo?	Are you allergic to anything?
¿Eres alérgico a algún medicamento?	Are you allergic to any medications?
¿Puedes tomar este medicamento?	Can you take this medication?
¿Tienes mareos?	Do you have dizziness?
¿Tienes náuseas?	Do you have nausea?
¿Has vomitado?	Have you vomited?
¿Qué síntomas tienes?	What symptoms do you have?
Tengo mareos	I'm dizzy
Tengo náuseas	I have nausea
Me duele la cabeza	I have a headache
Tuve un accidente	I had an accident
Me caí	I fell
Me rompí el tabique	I broke the septum
Te has fracturado la pierna	You have broken your leg

Te has fracturado el brazo	You have fractured your arm
Tienes que descansar	You have to rest
No hagas ejercicio	Don't exercise
No tomes alcohol	Don't drink alcohol
No fumes	Don't smoke
¿Tomas alcohol?	Do you drink alcohol?
¿Fumas?	Do you smoke?
¿Consumes drogas?	Do you use drugs?
¿Qué drogas consumes?	What drugs do you use?
Esta es la receta médica	This is the medical prescription.
¿Es usted el doctor?	Are you the doctor?
¿Puede ayudarme?	Can you help me?
¿Cuánto pesas?	How much do you weigh?
¿Cuánto mides?	How tall are you?
Siéntate aquí	Sit here
Recuéstate aquí	Lie here
Tienes que tener una cita médica	You have to have a medical appointment
Tienes que tomar este jarabe	You have to drink this syrup

Now that you have seen some common phrases, it's time to see some of those phrases in a conversation:

• ¡Buenos días!	• Good Morning!

• ¡Buenos días! ¿Este es el hospital Armando Plazas?	• Good Morning! Is this the Armando Plazas Hospital?
• Así es. Este es el hospital Armando Plazas. ¿En qué le podemos ayudar? ¿Tiene alguna emergencia?	• That's right. This is Armando Plazas Hospital. How can I help you? Do you have an emergency?
• No es una emergencia. Simplemente me duele mucho el estómago.	• It is not an emergency. My stomach just hurts a lot.
• Ya veo. ¿Tiene una cita médica?	• I see. Do you have a medical appointment?
• No	• No
• ¿Es la primera vez que viene a este hospital?	• Is it the first time you come to this hospital?
• Sí.	• Yes.
• Para ser atendido necesita tener una cita médica. Pero como a usted le duele mucho el estómago, usted puede ir a la sala de urgencias. Allí le ayudarán	• To be treated you need to have a medical appointment. But since your stomach hurts a lot, you can go to the emergency room. They will help you there
	• Thank you. Where is the emergency room?

• Gracias. ¿Dónd está la sala de urgencias?	• The emergency room is there.
• La sala de urgencias está allí.	• Thank you.
• Gracias.	• Is this the emergency room?
• ¿Es esta la sala de urgencias?	
• Sí. ¿En que le podemos ayudar?	• Yes. How can we help you?
• Me duele mucho el estómago.	• My stomach hurts a lot.
	• Have you eaten anything?
• ¿Ha comido algo?	• Yes.
• Sí.	• What did you eat?
• ¿Qué comió?	• I ate a plate of spaghetti in the street.
• Comí un plato de espagueti en la calle.	
	• Are you allergic to anything?
• ¿Es alérgico a algo?	• No.
• No.	• What symptoms do you have?
• ¿Qué síntomas tiene?	
• Tengo un fuerte dolor de estómago y también tengo náuseas.	• I have a strong stomach ache and I also feel nauseous.
	• Do you have dizziness?
• ¿Tiene mareos?	• No, I don't have dizziness
• No, no tengo mareos	

• Ok. ¿Tiene seguro médico?	• Okay. Do you have health insurance?
• Sí.	• Yes.
• Muy bien, señor. Le atenderemos en un momento. Siéntese aquí, por favor.	• Ok, sir. We will help you in a moment. Sit here, please.
• Ok. Muchas gracias.	• Okay. Thank you very much.

Let's take a look at another conversation:

• Gracias por la atención, doctor.	• Thank you for your care, doctor.
• No se preocupe. No olvide tomar sus pastillas.	• Don't worry. Don't forget to take your pills.
• ¿Cómo se llaman las pastillas?	• What are the names of the pills?
• Los nombres de las pastillas está en la receta médica que le di.	• The names of the pills are in the medical prescription I gave you.
• Hay muchos medicamentos escritos en esta receta médica.	• There are many medications written in this prescription.
• Así es. Estas pastillas son para el dolor de estómago. Tiene que tomar 1 pastilla	• That's right. These pills are for your stomach ache. You have to take 1

después del desayuno y una después de la cena.	pill after breakfast and one after dinner.
• Ok. Entiendo. ¿Y qué hay de este otro medicamento?	• Okay. I get it. And what about this other medicine?
• Ese es un jarabe. Ese jarabe ayudará con el ardor de garganta. Recuerde que tiene que tomarlo antes de comer.	• That is a syrup. That syrup will help with the burning sensation in the throat. Remember to drink it before eating.
• ¿Y estas pastillas?	• And these pills?
• Estas pastillas son para la infección.	• These pills are for the infection.
• ¿Algo más que deba saber?	• Anything else I should know?
• No debe comer nada picante. No debe tomar gaseosa o bebidas alcohólicas. ¿Usted fuma?	• You should not eat anything spicy. You should not drink soda or alcoholic beverages. Do you smoke?
• No, yo no fumo.	
• Bien. Usted no consume drogas, ¿verdad?	• No, I do not smoke.
• No consumo drogas, doctor.	• Good. You don't consume drugs, right?
	• I don't consume drugs, doctor.

• ¡Qué bien! No cene muy tarde. No se estrese demasiado.	• That's perfect! Don't have dinner too late. Don't get stressed out too much.
• ¿Puedo hacer deporte?	• Can I do exercise?
• Sí, pero con mucho cuidado.	• Yes, but very carefully.
• ¿Y si me vuelve a doler el estómago?	• What if my stomach hurts again?
• Si le duele mucho, entonces usted puede venir a la sala de emergencias.	• If it hurts a lot, then you can come to the emergency room.
• ¿Por cuánto tiempo debo tomar estas pastillas?	• How long should I take these pills?
• Debe tomar esas pastillas hasta la siguiente cita.	• You should take those pills until the next appointment.
• ¿Cuándo es la siguiente cita?	• When is the next appointment?
• La siguiente cita es en dos semanas.	• The next appointment is in two weeks.
• ¿Cuánto cuesta la cita?	• How much does the appointment cost?
• No cuesta nada. Su seguro cubre todas las citas.	• It costs nothing. Your insurance covers all appointments.

• ¿Qué más cubre mi seguro?	• What else does my insurance cover?
• Su seguro también cubre los medicamentos y cirugías, si es que lo necesita.	• Your insurance also covers medications and surgeries, if you need them.
• Muchas gracias por toda su ayuda doctor.	• Thank you very much for all your help doctor.
• De nada. Por favor, no se olvide tomar sus medicamentos.	• No problem. Please don't forget to take your medications.
• No lo olvidaré. Gracias.	• I won't forget. Thank you.

At the Pharmacy

After having been to the doctor's, you might need to go to the pharmacy to get the medication he prescribed to yo. What phrases can you use? Let's take a look at the most common:

Spanish	English
¿En qué le podemos ayudar?	How can we help you?
Quiero comprar estas pastillas	I want to buy this pills
¿Cuánto cuestan estas pastillas?	How much do these pills cost?
Quiero 20 pastillas	I want 20 pills
¿Quiere que le muestre mi receta médica?	Do you want me to show you my prescription?
¿Puede mostrarme su receta médica?	Can you show me your prescription?
Aquí está mi receta médica	Here's my prescription
¿Para qué sirven estas pastillas?	What are these pills for?

¿Tiene algún descuento?	Do you have any discount?
¿Desea comprar todos los medicamentos en esta receta?	Do you want to buy all the medication that's in this prescription?
¿Tiene esta receta médica la firma del doctor?	Does this prescription have the doctor's signature?
¿Cubre mi seguro estos medicamentos?	Does my insurance cover these medications?
Tengo seguro médico	I have medical insurance
¿Tiene medicamentos genéricos?	Do you have generic medications?
¿Tiene medicamentos de venta libre?	Do you have over-the-counter medications?
Quiero comprar medicamentos sin receta médica	I want to buy over-the-counter medications

Let's look at some conversations:

• ¡Buenas tardes!	• Good afternoon!
• ¡Buenas tardes! ¿En qué podemos ayudarla?	• Good afternoon! How can we help you?
• Quisiera comprar estos medicamentos.	• I would like to buy these medications.
• ¿Está es la receta médica?	• Is this the prescription?
• Sí, esta es la receta.	• Yes, this is the prescription.
• ¿Tiene la receta la firma del doctor?	• Does the prescription have the doctor's signature?
• Sí, aquí está firma del doctor	• Yes, here is the doctor's signature
• Muy bien. Nosotros tenemos todos estos medicamentos.	• Very good. We have all these medications.
• ¡Genial!	• Great!
• ¿Quiere comprar todos los medicamentos que se mencionan en esta receta?	• Do you want to buy all the medications mentioned in this prescription?
• No. Hay 5 medicamentos escritos ahí, ¿verdad?	• No. There are 5 medications written there, right?
• Sí. Hay 5.	• Yes. There are 5.
• Sólamente quisiera comprar 4.	• I would just like to buy 4.

- ¿Cuáles quiere comprar?
- Quiero comprar esta medicina. Son pastillas, ¿verdad?
- Así es. Son pastillas para el dolor de estómago
- Ok. También quiero comprar el jarabe.
- Este jarabe cuesta 50 dólares.
- ¿En serio? Pero solo quiero la botella de 150 miligramos.
- Lo siento. No vendemos ese jarabe en botellas de 150 miligramos.
- ¿En cuánto lo tiene?
- Sólo lo tenemos en 500 miligramos.
- Pero eso es demasiado.
- Lo sé, pero es lo único que tenemos.
- Bueno, entonces llevaré esa. ¿Para qué es ese

- Which ones do you want to buy?
- I want to buy this medicine. They are pills, right?
- That's right. They are stomach ache pills
- Okay. I also want to buy the syrup.
- This syrup costs $ 50.
- Really? But I just want the 150-milligram bottle.
- I'm sorry. We do not sell that syrup in 150-milligram bottles.
- What do you have?
- We only have it in 500 milligrams.
- But that is too much.
- I know, but it's the only thing we have.
- Well, then I'll take that one. What is that syrup for? I remember the

jarabe? Me acuerdo que el doctor me dijo que ese jarabe era bueno para la infección.

- Eso es cierto. Este jarabe es para la infección. ¿Qué otro medicamento quiere comprar?

- Quiero comprar este medicamento.

- ¿Cuál sería el último medicamento que comprará?

- Estas pastillas. Solo espero que no sean muy caras.

- No se preocupe, lo tenemos en genérico.

- ¿En serio?

- Así es. Si usted compra la version genérica de ese medicamento, le saldrá mucho más barato.

- Ok, suena bien. Quisiera llevar la versión genérica de

doctor telling me that syrup was good for the infection.

- That's true. This syrup is for infection. What other medicine do you want to buy?

- I want to buy this medicine.

- What would be the last medication you will buy?

- These pills. I just hope they are not very expensive.

- Don't worry, we have it in generic.

- Really?

- That's right. If you buy the generic version of that medicine, it will be much cheaper.

- OK, sounds good. I would like to have the generic version of that medication, then.

ese medicamento, entonces.	Very good. I see that you have medical insurance.
• Muy bien. Veo que usted tiene seguro médico.	• That's right.
• Así es.	• Your medical insurance covers all these medications. You will not have to pay absolutely anything.
• Su seguro médico cubre todos estos medicamentos. No tendrá que pagar absolutamente nada.	
• ¿En serio?	• Really?
• Así es.	• That's right.
• ¡Qué buena noticia! Muchas gracias.	• That is good news! Thank you very much.
• De nada, señorita.	• You're welcome.

Let's take a look at another conversation:

• ¡Buenos días!	• Good Morning!
• ¡Buenos días! ¿En qué podemos ayudarlo?	• Good Morning! How can we help you?
• Quisiera comprar unos medicamentos.	• I would like to buy some medications.
• ¿Tiene receta médica?	• Do you have a prescription?
• No, no tengo receta médica.	

Disculpe, sólo vendemos medicamentos con receta médica. No lo podemos ayudar.	No, I don't have a prescription.
Quiero comprar medicamentos de venta libre.	I'm sorry, we only sell prescription drugs. We can not help you.
Ya veo. ¿Qué medicamentos esta buscando?	I want to buy over-the-counter medications.
	I see. What medications are you looking for?
Quiero una pastilla para la gripe.	I want a flu pill.
	Do you have a cold?
¿Tiene gripe?	Yes
Sí	I get it. Here are some flu pills.
Entiendo. Aquí tiene unas pastillas para la gripe.	How should I take them?
¿Cómo debo tomarlas?	You should take one pill every eight hours. Don't drink alcohol or smoke.
Debe tomar una pastilla cada ocho horas. No tome alcohol ni fume.	I get it. How much do these pills cost?
Entiendo. ¿Cuánto cuestan estas pastillas?	These pills cost 8 dollars
Estas pastillas cuestasn 8 dólares	Does each pill cost 8 dollars?
	No, all pills cost $ 8.

• ¿Cada pastille cuesta 8 dólares?	• I get it.
• No, todas las pastillas cuestan 8 dólares.	• Anything else I can help you with?
• Entiendo.	• Well, I would also like to buy a stomach pain syrup.
• ¿Algo más en lo que le pueda ayudar?	• Ok, but you can only buy it if you have a prescription.
• Bueno, quisiera también comprar un jarabe para el dolor de estómago.	• Well, then I'll come back later with my prescription. Thank you
• Ok, pero sólo podrá comprarlo si tiene receta médica.	• No problem.
• Bueno, entonces regresaré luego con mi receta médica. Gracias	
• De nada.	

Short Stories

Exercises:

Read the following stories and then answer the questions. If you feel you don't understand the story, you can take a look at the translation of the story.

Now that you have learned the most common phrases to if you ever need to go to the mall, the doctor's, the gas station, the pharmacy and more, it's time that you see how you can get around a new place. In the next chapter, you'll learn even more phrases that will make you feel like a local wherever you go.

Yendo al centro comercial

Era un lunes cualquiera. Ariana se levantó muy temprano para ir a la escuela. Lo primero que hizo en la mañana fue tomar desayuno con sus padres y su hermano menor. Después de tomar desayuno, ella se vistió y fue afuera a esperar el bus.

El bus llegó en menos de cinco minutos. Ya dentro del bus, Ariana se encontró con sus amigas, Rocío y Fabiana. A pesar de que la semana recién ha comenzado, Rocío y Fabiana le dicen a Ariana para salir esa misma tarde al centro comercial. Ariana les dice que ella está muy ocupada como para ir de compras, pero sus amigas le dicen que el día de hoy habrá muchísimas ofertas y ellas no pueden perdérselas.

Ariana se pone a pensar por un momento. Ella sabe muy bien que tiene que hacer mucha tarea, pero a la vez sabe que las ofertas sólo estarán disponibles hoy día. Muchas de las cosas que se venden en el centro comerial son carísimas, así que tal vez hoy día sea el único día en que Ariana y sus amigas puedan comprar lo que quieran.

Ariana decide ir con ellas. Después de pedirle permiso a su mamá, ella llama a sus amigas para que la recojan. En sólo unos cuantos minutos, ellas llegan al centro comercial. ¿Qué es lo que Ariana y sus amigas quieren comprar?

El centro comercial es enorme. Es el centro comercial más grande de toda la ciudad. En realidad, este centro comercial es nuevo. Tal vez te preguntas dónde iban las personas a comprar. Antes de que este centro comercial abriera, las personas tenían que ir a otra ciudad si querían comprar cosas costosas como televisores, radios, celulares e incluso materiales de construcción. La ciudad más cercana está a una hora, así que las personas podían perder mucho tiempo tan sólo tratando de llegar a ese otro centro comercial.

Ariana y sus amigas están muy contentas de tener este centro comercial tan cerca de sus casas. Ahora que han entrado, ellas buscan las tiendas donde quieren comprar. Este centro comercial tiene tres pisos, así que será una aventura para ellas.

Going to the mall

It was a normal Monday. Ariana got up very early to go to school. The first thing she did in the morning was to have breakfast with her parents and her younger brother. After having breakfast, she got dressed and went outside to wait for the bus.

The bus arrived in less than five minutes. Already inside the bus, Ariana met her friends, Rocío and Fabiana. Although the week has just begun, Rocío and Fabiana tell Ariana to go to the mall that afternoon. Ariana tells them that she is too busy to go shopping, but her friends tell her that today there will be many offers and they cannot miss them.

Ariana starts thinking for a moment. She knows very well that she has to do a lot of homework, but at the same time she knows that the offers will only be available today. Many of the things sold in the mall are very expensive, so maybe today is the only day in which Ariana and her friends can buy whatever they want.

Ariana decides to go with them. After asking her mother for permission, she calls her friends to pick her up. In just a few minutes, they arrive at the mall. What do Ariana and her friends want to buy?

The mall is huge. It is the largest mall in the entire city. Actually, this mall is new. Maybe you wonder where people used to go shopping. Before this mall opened, people had to go to another city if they wanted to buy expensive things like televisions, radios, cell phones, and even building materials. The nearest city is an hour away, so people could waste a lot of time just trying to get to that other mall.

Ariana and her friends are very happy to have this mall so close to their homes. Now that they have entered, they look for the stores where they want to shop. This mall has three floors, so it will be an adventure for them.

Now that you have read the story, try to answer the following questions:

1. ¿A dónde van Ariana y sus amigas?

2. ¿Por qué no quiere Ariana ir con sus amigas al centro comercial?

3. ¿Quiénes son las amigas de Ariana?

4. ¿Por qué las amigas de Ariana quieren ir al centro comercial?

5. ¿Es nuevo el centro comercial?

Comprando nueva ropa

Ariana y sus amigas finalmente llegaron al centro comercial y ellas no pueden contener su emoción. Ellas ven que el centro comercial está muy decorado. En todos lados hay muchas personas. Hay muchísimas personas. Hay niños, adultos e incluso mascotas.

Rocío, una de las amigas de Ariana, sabe muy bien que quiere comprar. Ella quiere comprar un vestido largo. El vestido que ella quiere comprar cuesta más de 200 dólares pero hoy día, debido a los descuentos, ese vestido ahora cuesta sólo 50 dólares. Por ello, Rocío va a la tienda de ropa lo más rápdio que puede. En realidad, ella corre hacia la tienda. Ariana y Fabiana tiene que seguirla si no quieren quedarse sólas.

Cuando Rocío llega a la tienda, ella ve que hay muchas personas dentro de la tienda de ropa. Ella no sabe que hacer. Ella ve el vestido que quiere. El vestido que ella quiere viene en varios colores. ¿Cuál color le quedará mejor? Para saber qué color le queda mejor, ella se prueba todos los vestidos que hay disponibles.

Fabiana y Ariana se quedan sentadas esperándola afuera de los probadores. Ellas no pueden creer cuento tiempo le toma a Rocío decidirse por un color de vestido. Al final, ella no sabe qué color escoger y le pregunta a sus amigas. ¿Qué es lo que ellas dicen?

Ellas le dicen que ella debe comprar el vestido de color azul. A ella le encanta la idea y se lo compra. Ahora sólo falta pagar por el vestido. Felizmente, Rocío tiene su tarjeta de crédito. Si ella usa su tarjeta de crédito, ella tendrá incluso más descuentos disponibles.

Ariana quiere comprar un cargador de celular. ¿Dónde puede conseguir un cargador de celular? En la tienda de elctrónicos, ¡por supuesto! Como Fabiana también quiere comprar unos nuevos audífonos, ella decide ir con ella. ¿Qué hay de Rocío? Ella no quiere ir porque piensa que ir a la tienda de electrónicos es muy aburrido. Por ello, Rocío se queda tomando un café cerca de la tienda de ropa.

Ariana encuentra el cargador que quiere, pero desafortunadamente, ese cargador no tiene nigún descuento. Lo bueno es que ella al menos no necesitará gastar mucho dinero ya que ese cargador no está tan caro. Fabiana, por su parte, va a buscar los audífonos que ella quiere comprar. Ella vio los audífonos que quiere comprar en televisión. Son muy caros pero ella piensa que ahora de seguro el precio habrá bajado debido a los descuentos.

Fabiana estaba en lo cierto. ¡Los audídfonos que ella quiere comprar no cuestan casi nada! Fabiana no lo piensa mucho y los compra de inmediato. La única persona que no compra nada es Ariana. A pesar de que el cargador de celular que ella encontró es barato, ella no lo quiere comprar porque no tiene suficiente dinero.

Lo bueno de tener amigas es que, a veces, ellas te ayudan si tú necesitas algo. En este caso, Ariana necesitaba dinero para comprar el cargador y sus amigas quieren ayudarla a comprárselo. Fabiana y Rocío dan a Ariana el dinero que necesita para comprar el cargador y ella les agradece. Al final, todos salen del centro comercial muy contentos.

Buying new clothes

Ariana and her friends finally arrived at the mall, and they can't contain their excitement. They see that the mall is very decorated. Everywhere, there are many people. There are many people. There are children, adults, and even pets.

Rocío, one of Ariana's friends, knows very well what she wants to buy. She wants to buy a long dress. The dress she wants to buy costs more than $ 200 but today, due to the discounts that dress now costs only $ 50. Therefore, Rocío goes to the clothing store as quickly as possible. Actually, she runs to the store. Ariana and Fabiana have to follow her if they don't want to stay alone.

When Rocío arrives at the store, she sees that there are many people inside the clothing store. She doesn't know what to do. She sees the dress she wants. The dress she wants comes in several colors. Which color will fit her best? To find out which color suits her best, she tries on all the dresses that are available.

Fabiana and Ariana sit around, waiting for her outside the changing rooms. They can't believe how long it takes Rocío to decide on a dress color. In the end, she doesn't know what color to choose and asks her friends. What do they say?

They tell her that she should buy the blue dress. She loves the idea and buys it. Now she just needs to pay for the dress. Happily, Rocío has here credit card. If she uses her credit card, she will have even more discounts available.

Ariana wants to buy a cell phone charger. Where can she get a cell phone charger? In the electronics store, of course! As Fabiana also wants to buy some new headphones, she decides to go with her. What about Rocío? She doesn't want to go because she thinks that going to the electronics store is very boring. So, Rocío stays and drinks coffee near the clothing store.

Ariana finds the charger she wants, but unfortunately, that charger has no discount. The good thing is that she at least will not need to spend a lot of money since that charger is not so expensive. Fabiana, meanwhile, is looking for the headphones she wants to buy. She saw the headphones she wants to buy on television. They are very expensive, but she thinks that now the price will surely have dropped due to discounts.

Fabiana was right. The headphones she wants to buy cost almost nothing! Fabiana doesn't think too much and buys them immediately. The only person who doesn't buy anything is Ariana. Although the cell phone charger she found is cheap, she doesn't want to buy it because she doesn't have enough money.

The good thing about having friends is that sometimes they help you if you need anything. In this case, Ariana needed money to buy the charger, and her friends want to help her buy it. Fabiana and Rocío give Ariana the money she needs to buy the charger and she thanks them. In the end, everyone leaves the mall very happy.

Now that you have read the story, try to answer the following questions:

1. ¿Qué es lo primero que Ariana y sus amigas notan al llegar al centro comercial?

2. ¿Qué es lo que Rocío quiere comprar?

3. ¿Por qué Rocío se toma mucho tiempo en los cambiadores?

4. ¿Cuánto cuesta ahora el vestido que Rocío quiere comprarse?

5. ¿De qué color es el vestido que Rocío compra?

6. ¿Cómo paga Rocío?

7. ¿Qué es lo que Ariana quiere comprar?

8. ¿Qué es lo que Fabiana quiere comprar?

9. ¿A qué tienda Ariana y Fabiana van para comprar lo que ellas quieren?

10. ¿Por qué Rocío no quiere ir a la tienda de electrónicos?

11. ¿Por qué Ariana no puede comprar el cargador de celular?

12 ¿Cómo logra Ariana comprar el cargador de celular?

Obteniendo una tarjeta de débito

Raúl está yendo al banco que está cerca del aeropuerto. ¿Por qué está él yendo al banco? Porque él quiere obtener una tarjeta de débito. Él sabe muy bien que para obtener una tarjeta de débito, él necesita presentar muchos documentos. Por eso, si tú lo vieses en la calle, lo verías con muchos papeles en las manos. ¿Le servirán todos esos papeles para obtener la tarjeta de débito?

Raúl estaciona su auto y después de estacionarlo, baja y cierra la puerta. Él se da cuenta de que no le queda mucha gasolina, pero no se preocupa demasiado. Al momento de entrar al banco, una persona muy amable le saluda:

"¡Hola! ¿Cómo está?" – pregunta una persona

"Estoy muy bien" – responde Raúl, un poco nervioso

"Soy trabajadora de este banco. ¿En qué le podemos ayudar esta tarde?"

"Quisiera obtener una tarjeta de débito"

"Ha venido al lugar indicado para ello, señor. Tome este ticket y espere su turno, por favor."

"Gracias"

Raúl se sienta y espera a que lo llamen. Él pensaba que él iba a esperar por horas, pero en realidad lo llamaron en menos de cinco minutos. Raúl, contento, se levanta e inmediatamente va hacia la ventanilla.

En la ventanilla hay otro trabajador del banco. Raúl lo saluda y le dice lo que ha venido a hacer en ese banco. El trabajador del banco lo escucha y le dice que le puede ayudar con eso. El trabajador del banco le pide un poco de información a Raúl. ¿Qué información le pide a Raúl?

Lo que el trabajador le pide a Raúl es muy simple. Primero, un documento de identidad. Un documento de identidad puede ser un pasaporte o una licencia de conducir. Luego,

Raúl tiene que mostar papeles que demuestren que él ha estado trabajando por cierto tiempo.

Finalmente, le piden su dirección. Raúl tiene todos esos papeles así que no es nada difícil para él presentarlos. Lo único difícil será esperar. Raúl no es una persona muy paciente así que a él no le gusta esperar.

Si él quiere obtener su tarjeta de débito, entonces tendrá que esperar 2 semanas. Su tarjeta le llegará en el correo en dos semanas. Toda la información sobre su nueva tarjeta también le llegará en el mismo sobre donde estará su tarjeta.

A pesar de que a Raúl no le gusta la idea de esperar dos semanas, él se siente emocionado ya que por fin tendrá su propia tarjeta. Alegre, él sube a su auto y empieza a regresar a casa. El carro tiene algunos problemas y no enciende fácilmente. Es allí cuando Raúl se da cuenta que necesita ir a una gasolinera lo más pronto posible.

Getting a debit card

Raul is going to the bank that is near the airport. Why is he going to the bank? Because he wants to get a debit card. He knows very well that to get a debit card, he needs to present many documents. Therefore, if you saw him on the street, you would see him with many papers in his hands. Will all those papers be useful to get the debit card?

Raúl parks his car, and after parking it, he gets off and closes the door. He realizes he doesn't have much gas left, but he doesn't worry too much. Upon entering the bank, a very kind person greets him:

"Hi! How are you? "- asks a person

"I am very well" - Raúl replies, a little nervous

"I am a worker at this bank. How can we help you this afternoon? "

"I would like to get a debit card"

"You have come to the right place for that, sir. Take this ticket and wait for your turn, please. "

"Thank you"

Raul sits down and waits for him to be called. He thought he was going to wait for hours, but they actually called him in less than five minutes. Raul, happy, gets up, and immediately goes to the window.

In the window, there is another bank worker. Raul greets him and tells him what he has come to do in that bank. The bank worker listens to him and tells him that he can help him with that. The bank worker asks Raul for some information. What information does he ask Raul?

What the worker asks Raul is very simple. First, an identity document. An identity document can be a passport or a driver's license. Then, Raul has to show some papers that show that he has been working for some time.

Finally, they ask for his address. Raul has all those papers, so it is not difficult for him to present them. The only difficult thing will be to wait. Raúl is not a very patient person so he doesn't like to wait.

If he wants to get his debit card, then he will have to wait for 2 weeks. His card will arrive in the mail in two weeks. All the information about his new card will also arrive in the same envelope, one where his card will be.

Although Raul does not like the idea of waiting for two weeks, he feels excited because he will finally have his own card. Cheerful, he gets in his car and begins to get back home. The car has some problems and does not start easily. That's when Raúl realizes he needs to go to a gas station as soon as possible.

Now that you have read this story, try to answer the following questions:

1. ¿A dónde va Raúl para conseguir una tarjeta de débito?

2. ¿Qué documentos tiene Raúl que presentar?

3. ¿Cuánto tiempo tendrá que esperar Raúl para recibir su tarjeta de débito?

4. ¿Cómo se siente Raúl después de haber obtenido su tarjeta de débito?

En la gasolinera

Raúl finalmente llega a la gasolinera después de haber conducido por diez minutos. Él no conoce mucho esa zona. Él vive muy lejos del aeropuerto así que no sabe donde están las gasolineras.

Cerca del aerpuerto hay muchas gasolineras, así que él no tiene que ir tan lejos. Al llegar a la gasolinera, él le pide al trabajador que ponga en su auto 10 litros de gasolina.

Eso parece mucha gasolina, pero Raúl la necesita. Él trabaja como taxista, así que él conduce muchísimo. Hace unos días, él tuvo que recorrer casi toda la ciudad. Hoy día él sólo trabajará 5 horas, pero de todos modos necesitará mucha gasolina.

¿Cuánto le costarán 10 litros de gasolina? Él lo sabe muy bien. Por eso, no se sorprende cuando el trabajador de la gasolinera le dice que 10 litros de gasolina son 30 dólares. Lo que sorprende a Raúl es escuchar al trabajador de la gasolinera decir que hay un descuento especial si él paga con tarjeta de débito.

¿Qué puede Raúl decir? ¿Le dirá que su tarjeta de débito la tendrá en 2 semanas? Obviamente el trabajador de la gasolinera no le creerá. Lo que es más, él necesita la gasolina ahora mismo, no en 2 semanas. Si él no consigue la gasolina ahora mismo, no podrá llegar a casa.

Raúl no tiene más opción que pagar el precio normal por la gasolina. Después de llenar el tanque, él regresa a casa. Su familia lo ha estado esperando toda la tarde. Su esposa sabe muy bien la razón por la cual el fue a obtener una tarjeta de débito. Él necesitaba la tarjeta para obtener el descuento en gasolina. Él lo necesita, después de todo, él trabaja como taxista.

At the gas station

Raul finally arrives at the gas station after driving for ten minutes. He doesn't know that area very much. He lives far from the airport, so he doesn't know where the gas stations are.

There are many gas stations near the airport, so he doesn't have to go that far. Upon arriving at the gas station, he asks the worker to put 10 liters of gasoline in his car.

That seems like a lot of gasoline, but Raul needs it. He works as a taxi driver, so he drives a lot. A few days ago, he had to drive through almost the entire city. Today he will only work for 5 hours, but he will still need a lot of gas anyway.

How much will 10 liters of gasoline cost him? He knows it very well. Therefore, he is not surprised when the gas station worker tells him that 10 liters of gasoline is 30 dollars. What surprises Raul is to hear the gas station worker say that there is a special discount if he pays with a debit card.

What can Raul say? Will he tell him that he will have his debit card in 2 weeks? Obviously, the gas station worker will not believe him. What's more, he needs gasoline right now, not in 2 weeks. If he doesn't get gas right now, he won't be able to get home.

Raul has no choice but to pay the normal price for gasoline. After filling the tank, he returns home. His family has been waiting for him all afternoon. His wife knows very well the reason he went to get a debit card. He needed the card to get the discount on gas. He needs it; after all, he works as a taxi driver.

Now that you have read the story, try to answer the following questions:

1. ¿Cuántos litros de gasoline pide Raúl?

2. ¿A qué se dedica Raúl?

3. ¿Cuántas horas trabajará Raúl hoy día?

4. ¿Cómo puede Raúl conseguir el descuento especial en gasolina?

5. ¿Quién más sabe porque Raúl decidió obtener una tarjeta de débito?

Chapter 4: Common Travel Phrases

Calling a Taxi

When you travel to a new place, it might be hard to get around at first. Some of the most common means of transportation in a city are buses and private cars. Some private cars, though, can also be used as taxis. They will be waiting for you everywhere: at the airport, at the mall, at the hospital, even outside schools. Let's see the most common phrases you can use to get a taxi:

1.	¿Dónde puedo pedir un taxi?
2.	Ese es el taxi que quiero tomar
3.	No me gusta este taxi
4.	Este taxi es muy grande

5.	No vamos a entrar en este taxi
6.	Me gusta este taxi
7.	¿Este taxi tiene seguro?
8.	¿Cuál es el nombre del conductor de este taxi?
9.	¿Dónde está el conductor de este taxi?
10.	¿Cuánto cuesta llegar hasta el aeropuerto?
11.	¿Cuánto cuesta llegar hasta el centro comercial?
12.	No sé cómo llegar al centro comercial
13.	No sé cómo llegar al aeropuerto
14.	¿Cuesta mucho llegar al aeropuerto?
15.	¿Cuesta mucho llegar al centro comercial?
16.	¿Cómo se llama?

And this is the translation

1.	Where can I call a taxi?
2.	That's the taxi I want to take
3.	I don't like this taxi
4.	This taxi is very big
5.	We're not going to fit into this taxi
6.	I like this taxi
7.	Does this taxi have insurance?
8.	What's the name of the driver of this taxi?
9.	Where's the driver of this taxi?
10.	How much does the ride to the airport cost?
11.	How much does the ride to the airport cost?

12. I don't know how to get to the mall
13. I don't know how to get to the airport
14. Does it cost too much to get to the airport?
15. Does it cost too much to get to the mall?
16. What's your name?

Let's see some conversations where these phrases are used:

- ¡Buenas tardes!
- ¡Buenas tardes!
- ¿Es usted taxista?
- Sí, yo soy taxista. ¿Le puedo ayudar en algo?
- Sí. Quiero ir al aeropuerto. Yo no sé cómo llegar.
- No se preocupe. Yo le puedo llevar al aeropuerto.
- ¿Cuánto costará el viaje al aeropuerto?
- Le costará 35 dólares.
- ¿35 dólares? ¿No es eso demasiado?
- Está 35 dólares porque hay mucho tráfico.
- Pero el aeropuerto está a sólo 20 minutos de aquí.
- El aeropuerto está a 30 minutos de aquí en realidad. Recuerde también que hay muchas construcciones en las carrateras.
- Lo sé. Bueno, creo que no hay otra manera de llegar al aeropuerto.

- Así es. No hay buses disponibles porque ya es muy tarde.
- Bueno, entonces vamos. No esperemos a que se haga más tarde.

- Good afternoon!
- Good afternoon!
- Are you a taxi driver?
- Yes, I am a taxi driver. How can I help you?
- Yes. I want to go to the airport. I do not know how to get there.
- Don't worry. I can take you to the airport.
- How much will the trip to the airport cost?
- It will cost you $ 35.
- $ 35? Isn't that too much?
- It's $ 35 because there is a lot of traffic.
- But the airport is only 20 minutes from here.
- The airport is actually 30 minutes from here. Remember also that there are many constructions in the roads.
- I know. Well, I think there is no other way to get to the airport.
- That's right. There are no buses available because it is too late.

> - Well, then let's go. Let's not wait until it's too late.

Let's take a look at another conversation. In this case, the conversation is taking place between two friends who are trying to call a taxi through an app:

• ¿Qué estás haciendo?	• What are you doing?
• Estoy llamando a un taxi.	• I'm calling a taxi.
• Pero ya es muy tarde. No creo que haya taxis disponibles a esta hora de la noche.	• But it's too late. I don't think there are taxis available at this time of the night.
• No te preocupes. Tengo una aplicación que me permite llamar a un taxi sin tener que irme lejos de aquí.	• Don't worry. I have an app that allows me to call a taxi without having to go far from here.
• ¿En serio?	• Really?
• Así es. Mira, solo tengo que escribir a dónde quiero ir y la aplicación buscará a taxistas que quieran llevarme.	• That's right. Look, I just have to write where I want to go and the app will look for taxi drivers who want to take me.

- Suena bien, pero espero que no sea muy caro.
- ¡Para nada! No es tan caro cómo imginas.
- ¿Puedes mostrarme cómo funciona?
- ¡Claro! Mira, primero, abres la aplicación.
- Ok
- Después, tienes que escribir el nombre del lugar a dónde quieres ir.
- ¿También funciona si escribo la dirección de mi casa?
- Así es. Puedes escribir la dirección de tu casa. En este caso, yo escrbiré la dirección de mi casa porque es allí a dónde quiero ir.
- Ya veo. ¿Qué hay que hacer después?

- Sounds good, but I hope it is not very expensive.
- Not at all! It's not as expensive as you imagine.
- Can you show me how it works?
- Sure! Look, first, you open the app.
- Okay
- Next, you have to write the name of the place where you want to go.
- Does it also work if I write my home address?
- Yes. You can write your home address. In this case, I will write my home address because that is where I want to go.
- I see. What's next?

- Ahora sólo hay que esperar.
- ¿Esperar?
- Así es. Tenemos que esperar a que un taxista acepte.
- ¿Y si nadie acepta?
- No hay problema. Siempre hay muchos taxistas disponibles. Mira aquí en el mapa.
- Hay muchos carros.
- Así es. Todos esos carros son los taxis disponibles. Ya ves que que hay muchísimos.
- ¿Y cómo te das cuenta del precio?
- Solamente hay que mirar aquí.
- Ya lo veo. Ahí dice que el precio es 15 dólares. No es mucho. Es más

- Now I just have to wait.
- Wait?
- That's right. We have to wait for a taxi driver to accept.
- What if nobody accepts?
- No problem. There are always many taxi drivers available. Look here on the map.
- There are many cars.
- That's right. All those cars are available taxis. You see that there are many.
- And how do you see the price?
- Just see here.
- I can see that. There it says that the price is 15 dollars. It's not

barato de lo que pensé.

- Así es. Eso es lo que más me gusta de usar esta aplicación. Es muy barata.
- ¿Qué más puedes hacer en esta aplicación?
- Puedo pedir una van para que más personas viajen conmigo.
- ¿Y a qué hora viene el taxista?
- Mira, un taxista ya aceptó. Aquí dice que él vendrá en tan sólo 2 minutos.
- Ya veo. Ponte lista. Ya vendrá dentro de poco.
- Sí, lo sé.
- Tal vez también algún día use esa aplicación.

too much. It is cheaper than I thought.

- That's right. That is what I like the most about using this app. It is very cheap.
- What else can you do in this app?
- I can ask for a van so that more people can travel with me.
- And what time does the taxi driver come?
- Look, a taxi driver has already accepted. Here it says he will come in just 2 minutes.
- I see. Get ready. He will come soon.
- Yes, I know.
- Maybe one day I will also use that app.

• ¡Inténtalo! Verás que es muy fácil de usar.	• Try it! You will see that it is very easy to use.

Traveling by Plane, Bus and More

There's more than just one way to get to another country, but the most common, and easiest, is by plane. In this section, you'll learn phrases that will help you if you ever travel by plane to a Spanish-speaking country.

Spanish
1. ¿Dónde está el aeropuerto?
2. ¿Dónde puedo comprar un boleto de avión?
3. Quiero comprar un boleto de avión de primera clase
4. Quiero comprar un boleto de avión de clase económicoa
5. ¿Cuánto equipaje puedo llevar?

6. ¿Cuánto deben pesar mis maletas?
7. ¿Qué pasa si mi equipaje es muy pesado?
8. ¿Qué no puedo llevar en mi equipaje?
9. ¿Puedo llevar una botella de agua en mi equipaje?
10. ¿Puedo llevar esto en mi equipaje?
11. ¿Dónde quieres sentarte?
12. Quiero sentarme cerca a la ventana
13. Quiero un asiento junto a la ventana
14. Quiero sentarme cerca al pasillo
15. Quiero un asiento de pasillo
16. ¿Hay escalas en este vuelo?
17. ¿Cuánto dura este vuelo?
18. ¿A qué hora parte el avión?
19. ¿A qué hora aterriza el avión?
20. ¿A qué hora llegaremos?
21. ¿Cómo se llama esta aerolínea?
22. ¿Cuántas escalas hay?
23. ¿Dónde está compuerta?   ¿Dónde está la puerta?   ¿Dónde está la entrada?
24. El vuelo ha sido cancelado
25. El vuelo ha sido retrasado
26. Es hora de embarcar el avión
27. ¿Dónde está la salida de emergencia?
28. Esta es la puerta de la salida de emergencia

And this is the translation of the phrases:

English
1. Where's the airport?
2. Where can I buy a ticket plane?
3. I want to buy a first-class plane ticket
4. I want to buy an economic class plane ticket
5. How much luggage can I take with me?
6. How much does my luggage have to weigh?
7. What happens if my luggage is too heavy?
8. What can I not carry in my luggage?
9. Can I carry a bottle of water in my luggage?
10. Can I carry this in my luggage?
11. Where do you want to sit?
12. I want to sit near the window
13. I want a window seat
14. I want to sit near the aisle
15. I want an aisle seat
16. Are there layovers on this flight?
17. How long is this flight?
18. What time does the flight leave?
19. What time does the flight land?
20. What time will we arrive?
21. What's the name of this airline?
22. How many layovers are there?

23. Where's the gate?
24. The flight has been canceled
25. The flight has been delayed
26. It's time to board the plane
27. Where's the emergency exit?
28. This is the emergency exit door

Now that you have seen some phrases, take a look at some conversations where these phrases are used:

• ¿Qué estás haciendo?	• What are you doing?
• Estoy intentando comprar un boleto de avión.	• I am trying to buy a plane ticket.
• ¿A dónde estás pensando viajar?	• Where do you want to travel?
• Quiero viajar a España	• I want to travel to Spain
• ¿Ya sabes con que aerolínea quieres viajar?	• Do you already know which airline you want to travel with?
• No, aún no. ¿Puedes ayudarme? Tú viajaste a España el año pasado, así que estoy seguro que tú sabes dónde encontrar las mejores ofertas.	• No, not yet. Can you help me? You traveled to Spain last year, so I'm sure you know where to find the best deals.
• Creo que sí.	• I think so.

Spanish	English
• ¿Qué es lo primero que debo hacer?	• What is the first thing I should do?
• Primero, ingresa a la página web de una aerolínea.	• The first thing you should do is go to the website of an airline.
• ¿Qué aerolínea me recomiendas?	• Which airline do you recommend?
• Te recomiendo una aerolínea que se llama Iberia.	• I recommend an airline called Iberia.
• ¿Iberia?	• Iberia?
• Así es. Ese es el nombre de la aerolínea. Es una aerolínea que te puede llevar a España por precios muy baratos.	• That's right. That is the name of the airline. It is an airline that can take you to Spain for very cheap prices.
• ¡Genial! Ya encontré la página web de la aerolínea. ¿Qué debo hacer ahora?	• Great! I already found the airline's website. What am I supposed to do now?
• Ahora debes escribir el destino. ¿A dónde quieres ir?	• Now you must write the destination. Where do you want to go?
• Quiero ir a Madrid.	• I want to go to Madrid.
• Entonces escribe Madrid.	• Then write Madrid.
• ¿Y ahora?	• And now?

- Ahora debes indicar las fechas. ¿Cuándo quieres viajar?
- Quiero viajar el siguiente mes.
- ¿Cuándo piensas regresar?
- Quiero quedarme por 3 semanas. Así que regresaré después de 3 semanas.
- Ahora debes escoger el tipo de asiento que quieres. ¿Quieres un asiento de pasillo?
- Sí, quiero un asiento de pasillo.
- ¿Quieres un asiento en primera clase o en clase económica?
- Quiero un asiento en primera clase.
- Pero un asiento en primera clase puede ser muy caro.
- Lo sé, pero tengo el dinero para poder pagarlo.

- Now you must indicate the dates. When do you want to travel?
- 1 want to travel the following month.
- When do you think you will return?
- I want to stay for 3 weeks. So I will return after 3 weeks.
- Now you must choose the type of seat you want. Do you want an aisle seat?
- Yes, I want an aisle seat.
- Do you want a seat in first-class or economy class?
- I want a first-class seat.
- But a first-class seat can be very expensive.
- I know, but I have the money to pay for it.
- Okay. Very well. I think that would be all.
- Really?

• Ok. Muy bien. Creo que eso sería todo.	• Yes, now you just need to enter your credit or debit card information.
• ¿En serio?	
• Sí, ahora sólo falta poner la información de tu tarjeta de crédito o débito.	• Is that safe?
	• Yes, it is safe. I did it when I bought my plane tickets.
• ¿Es eso seguro?	
• Sí, es seguro. Yo lo hice cuando compré mis boletos de avión.	• I get it. I will do it right now, then. Thank you very much.
• Entiendo. Lo hare ahora mismo, entonces. Muchas gracias.	• No problem.
• De nada.	

Let's take a look at another conversation:

• ¿Qué estás haciendo?	• What are you doing?
• Estoy empacando.	• I'm packing.
• Pero tu vuelo es en dos días.	• But your flight is in two days.
• Lo sé, pero quiero tener todo listo para viajar.	• I know, but I want to have everything ready to travel.
• ¿Ya sabes lo que debes llevar?	• Do you already know what to carry?

- Sí. Tengo que llevar mi boleto de avión y también mi equipaje.
- No te olvides tu pasaporte.
- ¡Gracias! Casi me olvido de mi pasaporte. Creo que no me falta nada más.
- ¿Qué estás llevando en tu equipaje?
- Estoy llevando ropa, un cepillo de dientes, jabón y un perfume.
- No te olvides de llevar ropa interior.
- No me olvidaré. Gracias.
- ¿Qué es esto?
- Es un perfume. Es nuevo. Mi mamá me lo regaló la semana pasada.
- Pero no puedes llevar este perfume.
- ¿En serio? ¿Por qué no?
- Porque esta botella de perfume es muy grande.

- Yes. I have to take my plane ticket and also my luggage.
- Don't forget your passport.
- Thank you! I almost forgot about my passport. I think I don't need anything else.
- What are you carrying in your luggage?
- I am carrying clothes, a toothbrush, soap and perfume.
- Don't forget to carry underwear.
- I won't forget it. Thank you.
- What is this?
- It is perfume. It's new. My mom gave it to me last week.
- But you can't carry this perfume.
- Really? Why not?

- ¿En serio?
- Sí. Tú sólo puedes llevar botellas de 100 miligramos en ese vuelo.
- ¡No lo sabía!
- Lo que puedes hacer es conseguir otra botella de perfume.
- Entiendo. ¿Significa eso también que no podré llevar esta botella de agua?
- No podrás llevar esa botella de agua. Es demasiado grande.
- ¡Vaya! No sé que hacer.
- No te preocupes, solamente compra otra botela de agua más pequeña.
- Entiendo. ¿Algo más que deba recordar?
- No pierdas de vista tu equipaje. Ten mucho cuidado que no se pierda.

- Because this perfume bottle is very large.
- Really?
- Yes. You can only carry 100-milligram bottles on that flight.
- I didn't know it!
- What you can do is get another bottle of perfume.
- I understand. Does that also mean that I will not be able to carry this water bottle?
- You will not be able to carry that bottle of water. It's too big.
- Wow! I don't know what to do.
- Don't worry, just buy another smaller water bottle.
- I get it. Anything else I should remember?

• Gracias. Estoy muy emocionado por el viaje.	• Don't lose sight of your luggage. Be very careful not to lose it.
• Lo sé. Es la primera vez que viajas a España. Sé que lo vas a disfrutar bastante. No te olvides llamar cuando llegues.	• Thank you. I am very excited about the trip.
	• I know. It is the first time you travel to Spain. I know you will enjoy it a lot. Don't forget to call when you arrive.
• No me olvidaré. Gracias.	• I won't forget. Thank you.

By Bus

Traveling by bus is also very useful when you're living in a very big city. It can take you from one end of the city to another for a very cheap price. What should you know when traveling by bus?

Spanish
1. ¿Dónde está el paradero de buses?
2. ¿Funcionan los buses hoy día?
3. ¿A qué hora parte el bus?
4. ¿Cuánto cuesta el pasaje de bus?
5. ¿Necesito una tarjeta de bus?
6. El pasaje de bus es 1 dólar
7. No tengo suficiente dinero para el pasaje
8. ¿Vas a viajar conmigo?
9. ¿Dónde debo bajarme?
10. ¿Cuánto falta para llegar?
11. Falta 2 horas para llegar
12. Aún no llegamos
13. ¿Dónde está el chofer del bus?

English
1. Where's the bus stop?
2. Do buses work today?
3. What time does the bus leave?
4. How much is the bus fare?
5. Do I need a bus card?

6. The bus fare is one dollar.
7. I don't have enough money to pay the bus fare
8. Are you going to travel with me?
9. Where should I get off?
10. How long until we arrive?
11. We'll arrive in 2 hours
12. We haven't arrived yet
13. Where's the bus driver?

Let's take a look at some conversations where these phrases are used:

• Si quiero ir al centro comercial, ¿tengo que tomar un bus? • Sí. • ¿Puedo tomar cualquier bus? • No. Si quieres llegar al centro comercial, tienes que tomar el bus de color amarillo. • Ok, entiendo. Tengo que tomar el bus de color amarillo.	• If I want to go to the mall, do I have to take a bus? • Yes. • Can I take any bus? • No. If you want to go to the mall, you have to take the yellow bus. • Ok, I understand. I have to take the yellow bus. • You know how much the bus fare costs, right? • I don't know. How much is it?

- Sabes cuánto cuesta el pasaje de bus, ¿verdad?
- No lo sé. ¿Cuánto cuesta?
- El pasaje cuesta 2 dólares.
- Pero yo he escuchado que algunas personas pagan sólo 1 dólar o incluso menos.
- Debe ser porque esas personas son estudiantes. Los estudiantes pagan menos que las otras personas.
- Pero yo he visto a personas mayores pagando menos también.
- Eso es porque las personas mayores de 65 años pagan mucho menos que los demás también.
- Ok, entiendo.
- Recuerda que el paradero de bus dónde debes tomar el bus está en el parque.
- Gracias.

- The fare costs 2 dollars.
- But I have heard that some people pay only 1 dollar or even less.
- It must be because those people are students. Students pay less than other people.
- But I've seen older people paying less, too.
- That's because people over 65 pay much less than others, too.
- Ok, I understand.
- Remember that the bus stop where you should take the bus is in the park.
- Thank you.
- Don't sit on the red seats.
- Why not?
- Because those are reserved seats.

- No te sientes en los asientos de color rojo.
- ¿Por qué no?
- Porque esos son asientos reservados.
- Entiendo. ¿Cómo se llama el paradero dónde debo bajar?
- El paradero donde debes bajar se llama Supercentro
- Ok.
- Te tomará sólo 20 minutos en llegar.
- ¿En serio? Es muy rápido.
- Sí. El centro comercial está muy lejos pero el bus es muy rápido.
- Gracias.

- I get it. What is the name of the stop where I should get off?
- The stop where you must get off is called Supercenter
- Okay.
- It will take you only 20 minutes to get there.
- Really? It's very fast.
- Yes. The mall is far away but the bus is very fast.
- Thank you.

By Train

Traveling by train is also very common. While not all countries in Latin America have trains, this following vocabulary will surely help you if you find yourself in one of the countries where the train is the main means of transport.

Spanish
1. ¿Dónde está la estación de tren?
2. ¿Cuánto cuesta el ticket de tren?
3. ¿Es el tren rápido?
4. ¿Dónde puedo tomar el tren?
5. ¿Cuánto está la tarjeta de tren?
6. ¿Puedo comer en el tren?
7. No está permitido comer en el tren

English
1. Where's the train station?
2. How much is the train ticket?

3. Is the train fast?	
4. Where can I take the train?	
5. How much is the train card?	
6. Can I eat on the train?	
7. It's not permitted to eat on the train.	

Here's a conversation where you can see how these phrases are used:

• ¿Quieres ir conmigo al centro de a ciudad?	• Do you want to go with me to the city center?
• ¿Por qué vas a ir al centro de la ciudad?	• Why are you going to the city center?
• Hay un concierto. Muchas personas van a ir y yo también quiero ir.	• There is a concert. Many people are going and I want to go, too.
• Ya veo. Pero el centro de la ciudad está muy lejos. ¿Cómo vamos a ira allá?	• I see. But the city center is very far. How are we going to get there?
• Tomaremos el tren.	• We will take the train.
• ¿El tren? Yo nunca he tomado el tren.	• The train? I have never taken the train.
• ¿Nunca has tomado el tren?	• Have you never taken the train?

• Nunca he tomado el tren y tengo un poco de miedo.	• I've never taken the train and I'm a little scared.
• No te preocupes. No hay nada que temer. El tren es muy seguro.	• Don't worry. There is nothing to fear. The train is very safe.
• ¿Y es rápido?	• And is it fast?
• Sí que lo es. Viajar en tren es la manera más rápida que hay para llegar al centro de la ciudad.	• Yes, it is. Traveling by train is the fastest way to get to the city center.
• Sólo espero que no sea muy caro.	• I just hope it isn't very expensive.
• No es caro.	• It is not expensive.
• Pero yo he escuchado que hay que comprar una tarjeta de tren para poder entrar. Yo no tengo una tarjeta de tren.	• But I have heard that you have to buy a train card to enter. I do not have a train card.
• Lo sé. Por eso te voy a prestar mi tarjeta de tren.	• I know. That's why I'm going to lend you my train card.
• ¿En serio? Gracias. ¿A qué hora partiremos?	• Really? Thank you. What time will we leave?
• Partiremos a las 5 de la tarde. Si puedes venir conmigo, ¿verdad?	• We will leave at 5 in the afternoon. You can come with me, right?

• ¡Claro que sí! Yo también quiero ir al concierto.	• Of course! I also want to go to the concert.
• ¡Genial! Te espero en mi casa a las 4:30 de la tarde.	• Great! I'll wait for you at my house at 4:30 in the afternoon.
• Ok. Estaré ahí a esa hora.	• Okay. I will be there at that time.

Don't Get Lost

Asking for direction is a vital skill you'll need to learn whether you get to travel or not. Here are the most useful and common Spanish phrases you need to know:

Spanish
1. ¿Dónde estoy?
2. ¿Dónde estamos?
3. ¿Cómo llego al aeropuerto?
4. ¿Cómo llego al hospital?
5. ¿Cómo llego al centro comercial?

6. Estás perdido
7. ¿Dónde estás?
8. ¿Dónde puedo conseguir un mapa?
9. ¿Dónde está tu casa?
10. ¿Cuál es la dirección de tu casa?
11. ¿Cuál es la dirección de esta casa?
12. No sé la dirección de mi casa
13. Este es el paradero de bus
14. Tienes que seguir caminando
15. Tienes que ir a la derecha
16. Tienes que ir a la izquierda
17. El banco está al costado de la farmacia
18. La farmacia está al frente del hospital
19. La farmacia está a una cuadra de aquí
20. El banco está a dos cuadras de aquí

And this is the translation:

English
1. Where am I?
2. Where are we?
3. How do I get to the airport?
4. How do I get to the hospital?
5. How do I get to the mall?
6. You're lost
7. Where are you?

8. Where can I get a map?
9. Where's your house?
10. What's your home address?
11. What's the address of this house?
12. I don't know my home address
13. This is the bus stop
14. You have to keep walking
15. You have to turn right
16. You have to turn left
17. The bank is next to the pharmacy
18. The pharmacy is in front of the hospital
19. The pharmacy is one block from here
20. The bank is two blocks from here

Let's take a look at one conversation where these phrases are used:

• ¡Buenas tardes, oficial!	• Good afternoon, officer!
• ¡Buenas tardes! ¿Algo en lo que pueda ayudarla?	• Good afternoon! Anything I can help you with?
• Sí. No sé dónde estoy. Creo que estoy perdida.	• Yes. I don't know where I am. I think I'm lost.
• Ya veo. Bueno, este es el parque Ramón Buení. Este parque está en el centro de la ciudad.	• I see. Well, this is Ramón Buení Park. This park is in the center of the city.

• Entiendo. Pero yo quiero llegar al centro comercial.	• I get it. But I want to get to the mall.
• El centro comercial está en el otro lado de la ciudad. Si usted quiere ir allí, tendrpa que tomar el tren.	• The mall is on the other side of the city. If you want to go there, you will have to take the train.
• ¿Y dónde está el tren?	• And where is the train?
• El tren está a sólo dos cuadras de aquí.	• The train is only two blocks from here.
• ¿Podría decirme como llegar a la estación de tren?	• Could you tell me how to get to the train station?
• ¡Claro! ¿Tiene un mapa?	• Sure! Do you have a map?
• Sí. Tengo un mapa aquí.	• Yes. I have a map here.
• Muy bien. Estamos en este parque. ¿Lo puede ver?	• Very good. We are in this park. Can you see it?
• Sí. Puedo verlo claramente.	• Yes. I can see it clearly.
• ¡Genial! ¿Puede ver que hay un banco aquí?	• Great! Can you see that there is a bank here?
• Sí. Puedo verlo también.	• Yes. I can see it, too.
• Muy bien. Ese banco está al frente de la estación de tren.	• Very good. That bank is in front of the train station.
	• I see. And I can also see that the bank is very close.

• Ya veo. Y también puedo ver que el banco está muy cerca.	• That's right. You don't have to walk too much.
• Así es. No tiene que caminar mucho.	• Thank you very much, officer.
• Muchas gracias, oficial.	• No problem.
• De nada.	

Short Stories

Exercises:

Now that you have learned the most common phrases, try to read the following stories. After reading the stories, answer the questions that follow:

El conductor de taxi

Hace mucho tiempo que Juan no visita a su amigo, Mario. Juan tiene que ir a la casa de Mario pero no sabe cómo llegar ahí. Después de salir del aeropuerto, Juan tiene que decidir entre tomar un taxi o tomar un bus.

Como Juan no ha visitado esta ciudad por años, él no sabe si los paraderos de bus son los mismos que los de hace años. Ya que él no quiere perderse, él decide tomar un taxi. Para

429

tomar un taxi, él camina unos minutos más hasta llegar al lugar dónde todos los taxistas están.

Todos los conductores de taxi se dan cuenta que Juan quiere tomar un taxi. Juan se acerca a uno de los conductores y le pregunta si él lo puede llevar a la casa de su amigo. El conductor obviamente no sabe dónde está la casa del amigo de Juan, pero no hay problema. Juan le muestra al conductor del taxi la dirección de su amigo.

El conductor de taxi le dice que la casa de Mario está muy lejos y que podría costarle muy caro. Juan no tiene nigún problema. Él ya sabía que la casa de Mario está muy lejos del aeropuerto.

Ahora el conductor le dice a Juan el precio: 50 dólares. Eso le parece mucho a Juan pero no tiene otra opción. Juan sube al auto y el viaje empieza. Antes de llegar a la casa de Mario, Juan lo llama por teléfono y le pide que esté al tanto de su llegada.

The taxi driver

Juan has not visited his friend, Mario, for a long time. Juan has to go to Mario's house but he doesn't know how to get there. After leaving the airport, Juan has to decide between taking a taxi and taking a bus.

As Juan has not visited this city for years, he does not know if the bus stops are the same as those of years ago. Since he doesn't want to get lost, he decides to take a taxi. To take a taxi, he walks a few more minutes until he reaches the place where all the taxi drivers are.

All taxi drivers realize that Juan wants to take a taxi. Juan approaches one of the drivers and asks if he can take him to his friend's house. The driver obviously doesn't know where Juan's friend's house is, but there's no problem. Juan shows the taxi driver the address of his friend.

The taxi driver tells him that Mario's house is far away and that it could cost him a lot. Juan has no problem. He already knew that Mario's house is far from the airport.

Now the driver tells Juan the price: 50 dollars. That seems a lot to Juan but he has no other choice. Juan gets in the car and the journey begins. Before arriving at Mario's house, Juan calls him on the phone and asks him to be aware of his arrival.

Now that you have read the story, try to answer the questions:

1. ¿Cuánto le costará a Juan ir a la casa de su amigo?
2. ¿Cuál es el nombre del amigo de Juan?
3. ¿Está lejos la casa de Mario del aeropuerto?

Un nuevo chico en la ciudad

Diego acaba de llegar a una nueva ciudad. Él no habla mucho el idioma de la ciudad, pero él ha aprendido lo suficiente como para poder conversar con las personas que viven en esa ciudad. ¿Qué es lo que Diego está haciendo en esa ciudad?

Diego está visitando a su familia. Él se está quedando en la casa de su familia. A él le gusta visitar a su familia, pero a veces él tiene que esperar mucho tiempo para visitarlos ya que él trabaja casi todo el año. Además, es muy caro viajara a esa ciudad.

Mientras Diego esyá visitando la ciudad, él planea ir a algunos museos y también a los parques de diversiones. Hay tantos que a Diego no le alcanza el tiempo para visitar todos los museos. A Diego eso no le molesta. Él sabe que él puede volver el siguiente año para poder ver los museos que él no puede ver ahora.

Él a veces se pierde porque no conoce mucho la ciudad. Una vez, él casi se pierde ya que tomó el bus equivocado. Su tío tuvo que venir a recogerlo. Diego quería ir a un parque muy popular en el centro de la ciudad pero no se acordaba como llegar ahí. Él tomó un bus pero ese bus no era el correcto. El bus que Diego tomó lo dejó al otro lado de la ciudad; lejísimo del centro de la ciudad. A Diego no le quedó más remedio que tener que llamar a su tío para que venga a recogerlo.

En esta ocasión, Diego no se pierde, pero de todos modos tiene problemas para moverse en la ciudad. Los paraderos de bus han cambiado. Los paraderos de bus ya no son los mismos que los del año pasado. El tío de Diego le enseña como llegar al parque usando uno de los nuevos buses, pero tal parece que Diego no puede acordarse.

Diego no tiene ningún problema en llegar, pero ya se está haciendo tarde y él tiene que regresar a su casa. ¿Cómo lo hará? La respuesta es muy fácil. Diego coge su teléfono y esta vez llama, no a su tío, sino a su tía, para que lo recoja lo más pronto posible.

A new kid in town

Diego has just arrived in a new city. He doesn't speak much the language of the city, but he has learned enough to be able to talk with the people who live in that city. What is Diego doing in that city?

Diego is visiting his family. He is staying at his family's house. He likes to visit his family, but sometimes he has to wait a long time to visit them since he works almost all year. Also, it is very expensive to travel to that city.

While Diego is visiting the city, he plans to go to some museums and also to some amusement parks. There are so many that Diego does not have enough time to visit all the museums. That doesn't bother Diego. He knows that he can

433

come back the following year so he can see the museums that he can't see now.

He sometimes gets lost because he doesn't know much about the city. Once, he almost got lost since he took the wrong bus. His uncle had to come to pick him up. Diego wanted to go to a very popular park in the city center, but he didn't remember how to get there. He took a bus but that bus was not the right one. The bus Diego took left him on the other side of the city, far from the city center. Diego had no choice but to have to call his uncle to come to pick him up.

On this occasion, Diego is not lost but still has trouble moving around the city. Bus stops have changed. Bus stops are no longer the same as last year. Diego's uncle teaches him how to get to the park using one of the new buses, but it seems that Diego can't remember.

Diego has no problem arriving, but it is getting late, and he has to get back home. How will he do that? The answer is very easy. Diego picks up his phone and this time calls, not his uncle, but his aunt, to pick him up as soon as possible.

Now try to answer the following questions:
1. ¿Sabe Diego hablar el idioma de la ciudad?
2. ¿Cómo se perdió Diego?
3. ¿Qué planea hacer Diego mientras visita la ciudad?
4. ¿Quién ayudó a Diego cuando él se perdió?

5. ¿Por qué no puede Diego visitar a su familia a veces?

6. ¿Quién recoge a Diego en esta ocasión?

Conclusion

The Spanish language is not as difficult to learn as you think. This book *Spanish Made Easy* tried to live up to its name and tried to make the learning of this language something you can enjoy. What can you need to have in mind now that you learned the basics of this beautiful language?

This language, like any other language, has its complexities, and it can be a little frustrating for the reader to grasp these complex definitions and ideas. With that in mind, you need to know that learning a language might take more time than you think. Learning a language is a process and it takes time and effort to achieve fluency.

In the first chapter of this book, you've seen a detailed explanation of how the Spanish language works, and you can use it to try to comprehend how the language works. If you think the language is too difficult for you to understand or that a word is very complicated to pronounce, then you can take another look at this part of the book to remember how Spanish is structured and how it should be used.

In the second chapter, you've started to see the more difficult stuff: pronouns, verbs, and the comparative forms of adjectives and adverbs. This is what will really help you understand how the language is used by native speakers all over the world. All you learned in this chapter is just solidified by what you see next in the book.

In the third and fourth chapters, you've found the most common, useful, modern, and easy-to-understand phrases and terms used by Spanish native speakers in the world. The conversations that follow are just the icing on the cake. These conversations take into account your language skills. Also, you can be confident in learning these phrases because they are truly used by Spanish speakers. Learning to imitate the sounds and expressions that appear in the book will improve your vocabulary and your language skills

After reading the book, you know you can be satisfied to have learned what you need as a beginner. Now it's time to keep learning. Don't give up easily. Remember that learning a language takes time, but it surely delivers a lot of rewards. Don't forget to practice and remember that Spanish is a language that can be truly *made easy* to learn.

Made in United States
Orlando, FL
08 December 2024

55198349R00241